D0531222

Be a Super

Test-Taker!

THE ULTIMATE GUIDE TO
Elementary School
STANDARDIZED TESTS

Laurie Rozakis, Ph.D.

SCHOLASTIC REFERENCE

An Imprint of

SCHOLASTIC

www.scholastic.com

ACKNOWLEDGMENTS

Writing books is very hard work, so it's a good thing that many people helped me work on this project! I could not have done it without them.

My deep gratitude to my dear editor Mary V. Jones for accepting my idea and working with me to develop the format. Mary, you are not only one of the smartest people I know, but also one of the nicest.

A tip of the hat to the wonderful people in Scholastic's design department, especially Becky Terhune. Thanks, too, to Carol Bobolts of Red Herring, who created the beautiful page layouts and art. They are true artists. Great thanks to the proofreaders led by Susan Jeffers Casel, who caught all those errors that I should have caught. To all these dedicated professionals, I am indebted to your wisdom, expertise, and devotion.

Library of Congress Cataloging-in-Publication Data available

ISBN 10: 0-439-87879-9
ISBN 13: 978-0-439-87879-1

10 9 8 7 6 5 4 3 2 1   07 08 09 10 11

Printed in the U.S.A.
First printing, February 2007
Book design by Red Herring Design

Contents

Chapter 3
33 A Few Weeks Before Any Standardized Test...

Chapter 4
45 On the Day of Any Standardized Test...

Chapter 5
57 After Any Standardized Test...

Chapter 6
69 Deal with Test Worry

Chapter 7
77 Multiple-Choice Standardized Tests

Chapter 8
89 Short-Answer Standardized Tests

Chapter 9
101 Writing Essays on Standardized Tests

Chapter 10
113 Practice Standardized Tests

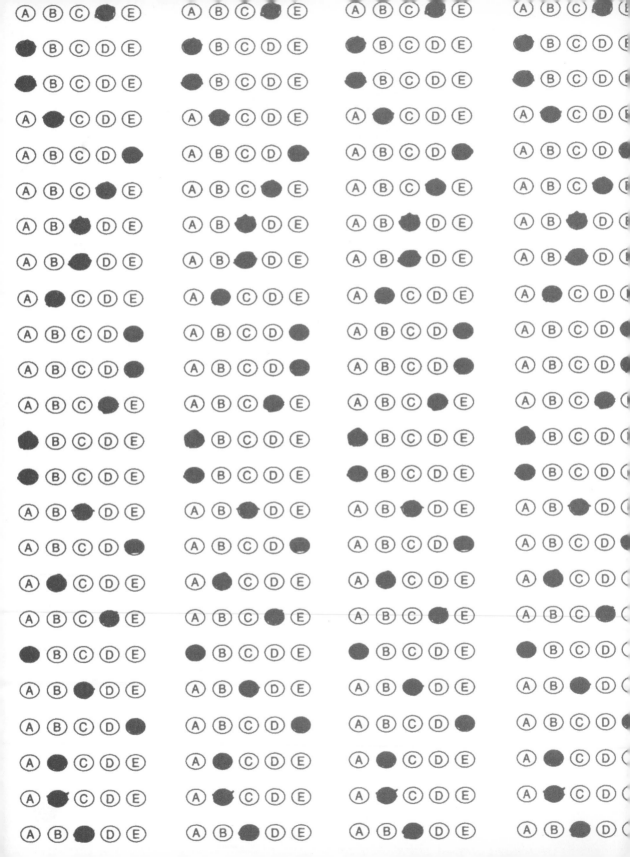

INTRODUCTION

Tests, tests, tests!

Take this test to see what you know about standardized tests.

Circle True if the sentence is true. Circle False if the sentence is false.

1. *States give standardized tests because they like to make students squirm.*
   TRUE   FALSE

2. *You should start studying for a standardized test the night before the test.*
   TRUE   FALSE

3. *After a standardized test ends, you don't have to think about it again.*
   TRUE   FALSE

4. *There's no way to reduce worry over a standardized test.*
   TRUE   FALSE

5. *All standardized tests are the same.*
   TRUE   FALSE

Every answer is false!

Here's the inside scoop.

1. States give standardized tests to find out what you understand . . . and what you don't understand. Then teachers use the test results to help you learn better. In **Chapter 1**, you will learn about some different kinds of standardized tests. You will learn why these tests are very important.

2. In **Chapters 2**, **3**, and **4**, you'll discover how to set up a study plan to prepare for a standardized test. You will learn how to get ready to do your best.

3. You can learn a lot from a standardized test. That's what you will find out in **Chapter 5**.

4. **Chapter 6** teaches you easy ways to deal with test worry. Staying calm and cool is super important when it comes to standardized tests. That's because these are high-pressure tests.

5. All standardized tests are not the same. Knowing how to prepare for each type of standardized test can help you do your best. That's what you will learn in the last part of this book. **Chapter 7** teaches you how to do your best on standardized tests that ask multiple-choice items. **Chapter 8** will help you ace standardized tests with short-answer questions. And **Chapter 9**? It's all about standardized writing tests.

This book will help you do your best on *all* standardized tests. And that's true!

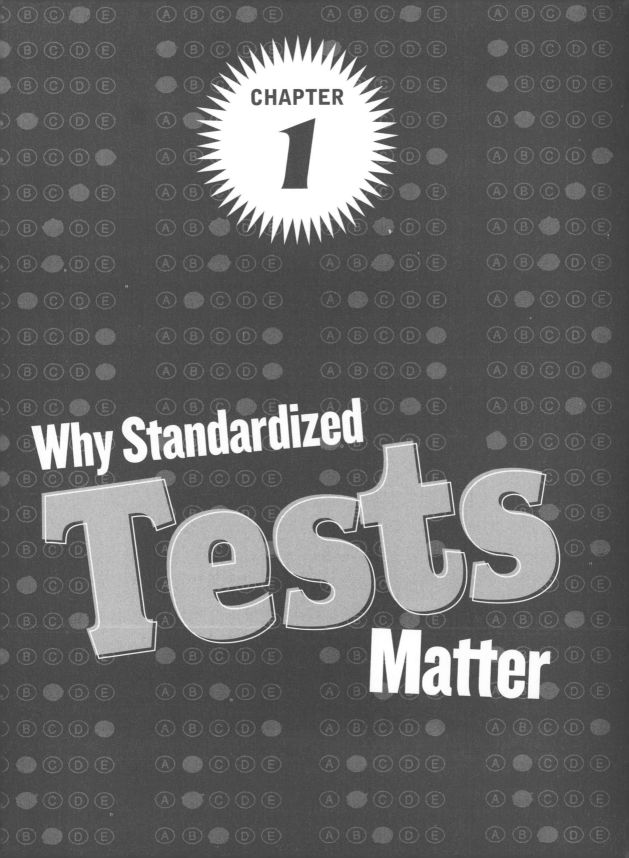

CHAPTER

1

Why Standardized Tests Matter

All tests measure what you know. You take many different kinds of tests. In school, you take classroom tests to see if you can add and subtract numbers. You take tests to see if you can find countries on a map. Some tests ask you to write an essay. Other tests find out if you can hit a ball. When you are older, you'll take a test if you want to get a license to drive a car.

How many times have you heard your teacher say, "Close your books. It's time for a surprise quiz!" Or how about, "Tuesday we'll have a test on units 1 and 2 in your social studies book." Maybe you've been told: "In May, you will take a standardized test." How are these tests the same? How are they different? Let's look at each type of test in detail.

Quizzes cover small amounts of material. A math quiz might cover one day's work. It might cover two pages. The quiz might take five or ten minutes to complete. Teachers write all the questions on a quiz. Teachers give quizzes to find out what you have learned before they move on. Sometimes, the teacher grades the quiz. Other times, the teacher might have students trade papers. The teacher reads the answers to the class and the students grade the papers.

Classroom tests cover more material. A math test might cover one week's worth of learning, such as one chapter or one unit. The test might take 30 minutes to complete. Teachers write all the questions on a test. Teachers give tests to make sure you understand a bigger chunk of material. The teacher grades tests.

Standardized tests are special kinds of tests. Standardized tests measure what you know as compared to a large group of kids your age. There are many ways that standardized tests are different from classroom tests.

For example, your teacher makes up a classroom test. But many people work together to write a standardized test. These people are not part of your school. They work for a company that designs tests.

your books!

Second, your teacher knows exactly what's on a classroom test.
After all, your teacher wrote the test! But your teacher does not know what's on a standardized test. Your teacher does not see the test before it is given. This means that your teacher can help you prepare for the test, but you have to do a lot of work on your own, too. Also, your teacher grades a classroom test. But machines grade standardized tests.

Next, standardized tests cover a lot of material.
A standardized test often covers a whole year's worth of work. It might even cover two or three years' work. Standardized tests are long, too. You may be given a whole morning to take a standardized test. Some standardized tests are given over an entire day or even a few days. Everyone in your state might take the same standardized test. Everyone in the country might take the same standardized test. They all take it on the same day, too.

Here's a huge difference: The tests count differently.
A classroom test counts toward your grade. It shows if you understand the material. A standardized test is used in other ways. It can show that a school is successful. It can show that a student is on grade level. It can show the opposite things as well. This is why standardized tests are called "high-stakes tests." **The "stakes"—the results— matter a lot.**

The following chart shows how classroom tests and standardized tests are the same and different.

CLASSROOM TEST	STANDARDIZED TEST
Written by your teacher	Written by a group of professional test makers
Tests one subject at a time	May test one subject or many subjects at a time
Your teacher can tell you exactly what will be on the test	Your teacher has not seen the test ahead of time. As a result, your teacher can't tell you exactly what information will be tested.
Taken by your classmates only	Taken by kids all over the country . . . maybe even the world!
Usually fairly short, perhaps 30 minutes	Often fairly long, perhaps a whole day or even two
Can be given any time	Given at the same time everywhere
Can take a make-up test or do a make-up assignment if you were absent	No make-up test
Graded by your teacher	Graded by machine
Counts in your grade	May count for many different things
Low-stakes test	High-stakes test

Below are the names of some standardized tests. These are given in elementary schools around the country.

California Standards Test
Early Childhood Literacy Assessment
English Language Arts Test
Florida Comprehensive Assessment Test
Iowa Tests of Basic Skills
Massachusetts Comprehensive
  Assessment System

Oregon State Assessment
Secondary School Admission Test
Terra Nova
Texas Assessment of Academic Skills
Texas Assessment of Knowledge and Skills
West Virginia Educational Standards Test

Why Standardized Tests Are Important

People are often afraid of standardized tests. They don't want to take them. Shhhhh…here's the big secret. Come closer. **Standardized tests are good.** How can that be?

Standardized Tests Help America

As you have already discovered, you take many different kinds of standardized tests in elementary school. Why are there so many standardized tests in elementary school? For starters, education is more important now than it's ever been before. People all over the world are competing with one another. As a result, schools are making sure you are receiving a great education. Standardized tests help them do this. This helps America stay strong.

Standardized Tests Help Schools

Second, standardized tests help other people find out if you have a certain skill. Teachers and schools use standardized tests to see what you have learned. Then teachers know what they have to go over in class. Standardized tests help teachers help you.

Standardized Tests Help You

Standardized tests help you get ready for middle school, high school, and college. They also help your parents know how you compare to other kids your age. This helps parents keep up with your learning. Even more important, standardized tests help *you* find out what you know. This helps you learn what you need to know to be an educated person. Most important of all, standardized tests help you learn what you need to make your dreams and goals come true.

> **STANDARDIZED TESTS are sometimes called *assessments*. "Assessment" is just a big word for "standardized test."**

Teachers have many ways to measure your progress. One of these ways is through standardized tests. Standardized tests also help get you ready for harder classes. They teach you to focus and study.

Standardized tests help you:
* ★ see what information you understand
* ★ see what information you don't understand
* ★ compare your progress to the progress of students your own age across the country
* ★ get into special programs
* ★ win contests
* ★ feel good about yourself

How Standardized Tests Show Only Part of the Picture

"I'll never be any good at standardized tests," you say. "My friend is better at standardized tests than I am." That may be true. Some people *are* better at standardized tests than other people. Why? It's because they know how to take standardized tests. They know how to study. They know how to stay calm during high-stakes tests. But don't worry: You will learn all this. You will get better at taking standardized tests. This will help you do better in school.

Most of all, remember that tests show only part of the picture about you.

Do Your Best on Standardized Tests

Follow these tips.

1. Like to learn.

"Broccoli is yucky," Jeff says. "I would never try it." How do you know you don't like something until you try it? School subjects are the same. Be open to trying new subjects. Enjoy learning new things. It's a lot easier to learn when you approach the subject with enthusiasm.

2. Make school your job.

Grown-ups go to their jobs every day. They get to work on time. They work a full day. They complete all their work. School is the same way. Right now, school is your job. Show up on time. Pay attention in class.

3. Enjoy school, but be serious about your studies.

School is fun. After all, you can hang out with friends, join clubs, and play sports. But school helps you learn many things you need. So have fun, but put your studies first.

4. Make up your mind to succeed.

"I'll never be good at math," Derek moans. "Math is hard, but I can learn it," Samara says. Which student do you think will have an easier time learning? It's Samara. You can talk yourself into doing poorly. You can also talk yourself into doing well. Go for the gold: Decide you will learn. Decide you are smart. It works!

5. Get extra help when you need it.

Teachers give extra help before school or after school. They can teach you the material one-on-one or in small groups. This often makes it easier to learn. Your older brothers and sisters can often help you, too. Your parents went to school. They know a lot of things! Ask them to go over the material with you before a big test. You can get help online, too. Special Web sites offer homework help.

6. Study for tests.

CASE #1: OWEN

Owen never studies for standardized tests. He figures that the answers will just come to him during the test. "It will be fine," he says. It rarely is. Owen does not do his best on standardized tests.

CASE #2: DAVE

Dave studies every day after school. He goes over what he learned that day in class. He also studies for all his tests, especially standardized tests. "I need to prepare," he says. "I feel more confident when I know all the information." Dave does very well on standardized tests. **"Dave is just smarter than me,"** Owen always says. Dave *is* smarter: *He knows that he has to study!*

There's nothing mysterious about Dave's success. It's a matter of hard work. It's not about being smart or not being smart. It's about being prepared. The process looks like this:

STUDYING = SUCCESS
ON STANDARDIZED TESTS

7 *Take care of yourself.*

You can't do your best if you haven't gotten enough sleep. How much sleep does the average elementary school kid need?

WRITE IN THE ANSWER:

The average elementary school kid needs _____ hours of sleep every night.

FIVE   SIX   SEVEN   EIGHT   NINE

Experts know that kids need at least **nine hours** of sleep every night. That's more sleep than adults need! (Adults need about eight hours of sleep a night.) You can't do your best in school if you're tired.

You can't do your best if you are not well, either. Getting enough sleep helps you fight off colds and other everyday illnesses. So does eating right, washing your hands, staying clean, and seeing your health care provider when you first get sick.

8 *Set good goals.*

School helps give you the skills you need to be a grown-up. Setting goals can help you remember that you are doing your best in school for a reason. Start by setting some school goals.

Here are some ideas:
* **Learn three new vocabulary words a week.**
* **Read one book for fun every week.**
* **Cut back on the time you play video games. Play only 15 minutes a day.**
* **Memorize two spelling words a day.**
* **Don't watch television while you're doing homework.**
* **Study math 15 minutes every day.**
* **Review social studies every night.**
* **Attend extra help twice a week.**

Later in this book, we'll talk about each of these tips some more. That's because they're so important.

set goals

Standardized Tests and You

How do you feel about standardized tests?

Take this test to find out. On the first list, circle the things you find easy. On the second list, circle the things you find hard.

WHAT I FIND EASY ABOUT STANDARDIZED TESTS	WHAT I FIND HARD ABOUT STANDARDIZED TESTS
1. Preparing for standardized tests	1. Preparing for standardized tests
2. Memorizing facts	2. Memorizing facts
3. Reading passages in standardized tests	3. Reading passages in standardized tests
4. Answering multiple-choice questions	4. Answering multiple-choice questions
5. Answering true/false questions	5. Answering true-false questions
6. Figuring out what the questions mean	6. Figuring out what the questions mean
7. Finishing the test in the time I have	7. Finishing the test in the time I have
8. Writing essays	8. Writing essays
9. Working at a steady pace	9. Working at a steady pace
10. Dealing with pressure	10. Dealing with pressure

How To Use This Book

There are many effective ways to make taking standardized tests easier. There are also effective ways to read books. **HERE'S HOW TO USE THIS BOOK.**

STEP #3
Underline important parts. Take notes on the main ideas.

STEP #1
Read the whole book. Read it from the start to the end.

STEP #2
Do all the exercises.

STEP #4
Look back at "Standardized Tests and You." Then go back over the book. Review the parts that match what you find hard to do on tests.

STEP #5
Skim the book before a standardized test. Use the study tips you need.

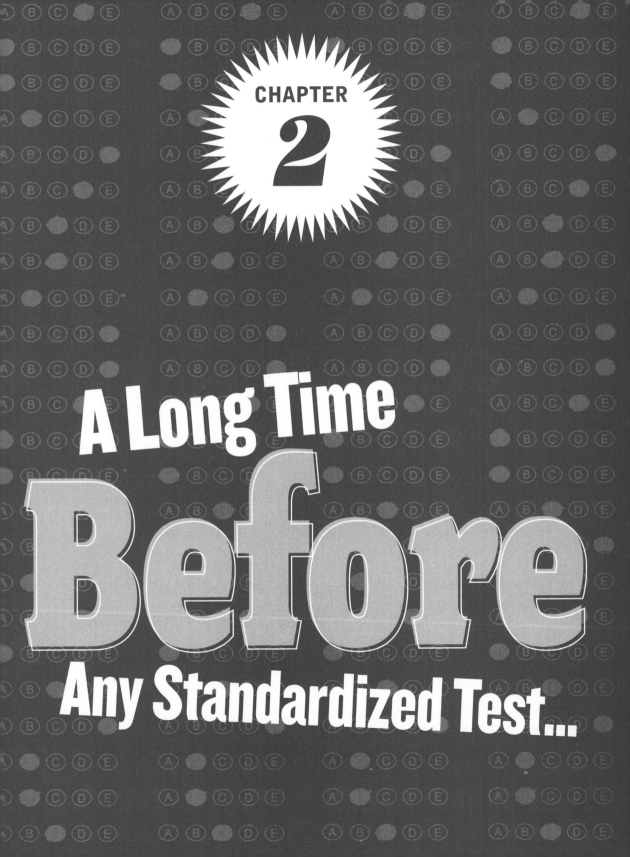

CHAPTER 2

A Long Time Before Any Standardized Test...

Which description best matches your mornings?

"Holly!" her mother yells. "Hurry up or you'll miss the school bus again." Holly jams an apple into her mouth and dashes out the door. The school bus is just pulling up. Holly jumps aboard. That's when she realizes that she has forgotten her backpack. Again.

Ennis has oatmeal and orange juice for breakfast. Then he kisses his family, picks up his backpack, and strolls to the school bus stop. "Five minutes early, as usual," his mother says as Ennis walks out the door. Ennis chats with his friends at the bus stop. On the way to school, he carefully reviews his notes for today's social studies test.

Let's make mornings easier for Holly! Getting a good start every day will make it easier for her to do well on her standardized tests. **That's because success on standardized tests starts long before the actual test. It starts with organization, studying, and preparation.**

Organize!

color is key

People say, "A place for everything and everything in its place." They're correct. Having all your school supplies in one place can make it much easier to do well. Having your class notes and handouts organized also makes it easier for you to study for standardized tests. Color coding helps a lot.

Classify Class Notes by Color

Get colored notebooks, highlighters, and folders. Choose one color for each class. For example, use blue for math, green for reading, and red for science. Write all your math notes in the blue notebook. Write all your reading notes in the green notebook. Write all your science notes in the red notebook, and so on. Your teacher may want students to get a specific kind of notebook. If so, get the notebook in the color you chose for each class. As you study in each notebook, highlight key points in the same color.

Get one notebook just for standardized tests. Put copies of already-given standardized tests in it. Write notes your teacher gives about upcoming standardized tests and keep them in there, too.

When you take notes, write the class and date on the top of the page. This will tell you when you took the notes.

Classify Handouts by Color

When the teacher gives handouts, put them in the notebook for that class. You can punch holes in each page and put the notes in your three-ring binder. Or you can staple the handouts to pages in your spiral notebook. Here's a third way: Place all the handouts in a folder color-coded to the subject, using the system that you have already established. For example, put your math handouts in a blue folder, your reading handouts in a green folder, your science handouts in a red folder, and so on.

Cover Books in Matching Colors

Cover your books in the same color. For instance, cover your math book in blue, your language arts book in green, your science book in red, and so on. Because everything is color-coded, you'll know which notebooks and textbook to take home with you every night.

Use an Assignment Book

Mark all your assignments in an assignment book. This is just a little notebook. You can also use a calendar. It works great! Include readings, homework assignments, quizzes, tests, papers, oral reports, and dates of standardized tests. Place a sticky note on a date when you'll be taking a standardized test. This helps you plan your time well so you can be all set for the test. Carry your assignment book with you all the time.

Prepare the Night Before a Standardized Test.

Getting all your stuff set up ahead of time can really help you calm down before a standardized test. Try these hints to get organized for the Big Day:

1. The night before any standardized test, check your assignment book. Make sure you know when the test will start and when it will end. Also check the place. Is the standardized test being given in the classroom or in a special room, like the gym? This way, you'll be on time and in the right place.

2. If you can bring a snack, pack it the night before.

3. Be sure to have at least two sharpened #2 pencils with erasers.

4. Check to see what other supplies you need. You might need a calculator, for instance. Be sure to check the batteries.

5. Pack your backpack the night before. Put it by the door.

6. Set out your clothes or uniform the night before.

Your turn: Write one way that you can get ready for a standardized test the night before:

....

....

relax

get ready!

Take Standardized Tests Seriously

Precious is taking a big standardized test in May. She starts studying in September. She studies every day. Great, right? Well, not so fast . . . Some days, Precious sits in the kitchen with her family and chats while she studies. Other days, she sits in the den and watches TV as she studies. She studies on the bus while talking on the phone and text-messaging her friends, too.

Flash forward to the day of the standardized test. Precious doesn't know most of the answers. "Why did I do so poorly?" Precious moans. "I *did* study! I studied for so loooonnnngggggg!"

No, she didn't study because she wasn't focusing on the material. Precious needed a study plan.

Here's how to create a study plan to prepare for standardized tests.

CREATE A STUDY SPACE
You need a quiet place to store all your schoolbooks, notes, and copies of already-given standardized tests. This place is called your study center. Your study center doesn't have to be big or fancy, but it *does* have to be the same place every day. A desk in your room, a desk in the attic or basement, and the reading room in the library all make good study centers.

FIND YOUR STUDY STYLE
Some students need complete silence when they study. Other students study better if quiet music is playing in the background. Some students study best on their own. Others often study best with friends. You'll study better if you match your study style to your personality.

STUDY THIS CHART TO SEE WHICH METHOD OF STUDY IS BEST FOR YOU.

STUDY ALONE IF YOU...	STUDY WITH FRIENDS IF YOU...
learn best through reading.	learn through listening.
need quiet to concentrate.	like to speak up in class.
don't enjoy group work.	are good at explaining things to others.
like to do things your own way.	can't sit still for long.
repeat material aloud as you study.	have friends who concentrate.

In general: ✷ turn off your iPod, radio, and television when you study; ✷ study on your own at least half the time; ✷ study at the same time every day. **Getting into a study routine lets your brain know when it's time to get to work.**

KEEP UP

One great way to prepare for standardized tests is to study tests that have already been given. Your teacher will often give you copies of these. But how can you get a copy of an old standardized test if you are absent? What can you do if you don't understand some questions on the test you're going over at home? There are several good ways to solve these problems.

Get a study buddy.

Choose a good student from your class to be your study buddy. Look for someone you can trust, someone who is well-organized. Then exchange telephone numbers and email addresses. Contact your study buddy if you missed class work or don't understand the assignment. It's a good idea to get at least three study buddies so you know you'll always be able to keep up with the work.

Check the class Web page.

Some teachers set up class Web pages. All the assignments, standardized test dates, and other special days are listed. Some class web pages also have links to good Web pages that offer homework help and links to old standardized tests. If your teacher has a class Web page, check it every day. This way, when something changes, you will know about it before class.

Email the teacher.

Some teachers want their students to contact them by email. Be sure to copy your teacher's email address down carefully. Send an email message before you need help so you know the email address works. Never contact your teacher by email if the teacher hasn't given permission.

Get Extra Help When You Need It

ask

Does this describe you?

Ariel finds math easy. He never has to study it. On Friday, the teacher covers a math concept that will be on the standardized test in June. Ariel doesn't understand it. "I always do so well in math," Ariel says. "But I can't learn this on my own. I know I need to know it to do my best on the standardized test at the end of the year. What should I do?"

Ariel should get extra help.

If you don't understand something in class, get help right away.

Always start by asking your teacher. List the topics that you don't understand. This will help the teacher help you. Bring your notes and books. Go over your notes, so your teacher can see if you copied something down incorrectly.

Next, you can ask your parents, grandparents, and older brothers and sisters for help. Your parents may know a lot about the subject. Your brothers and sisters may be able to explain it clearly to you, too.

Finally, get a tutor. Many schools have a tutoring center. It may be called a "Resource Room." You can ask teachers other than your own for extra help as well. Some schools will get you a tutor for free. You may even want to hire a tutor to go over the material with you a few times until you master it.

No matter who you ask for extra help, remember that you are asking for help. You are not asking them to do your work for you. That's not helping you at all!

Do All Your Schoolwork and Homework

Brianna is in the fourth grade. Every night, she gets about an hour of homework. She always has to do some math, science, and social studies. Once a week, she has to go over old standardized tests. But Brianna doesn't like homework. She has a lot of reasons why. "I need to practice playing soccer," she says. "I have to walk the dog," she tells her father. "Besides, I listen in class. I learn everything I need to know." "Then why did you do so poorly on the Terra Nova Standardized Test?" Brianna's father asks.

Why do teachers give homework?

Are they trying to be mean? No! Homework helps reinforce what you learn in class. It helps you figure out what you understand… and what you don't. Ever hear the old saying, "Practice makes perfect"? Homework is practice. It helps you understand the information you learned in class. It helps you remember important facts. It helps you learn what you need for standardized tests.

**Do all your schoolwork.
Do all your homework.
If this sounds like common
sense, it's because it is!**

reinforce what you learn at school

Be Serious About Standardized Tests

You read in Chapter 1 that standardized tests help our country, our schools, and *you*. That's why it's important to get into the right test mindset. Prepare a lot for every standardized test. Here's how:

1. *Keep up with the test news.*
Know when you have to take a standardized test. As you read earlier in this chapter, mark the test date in your assignment book or calendar.

2. *Study for the test.*
You learned this already, so it should be a breeze. Never go into a standardized test unprepared. Study pays off big time.

3. *Show up!*
This sounds silly, but some students stay home the day of a standardized test! "I'm too nervous," they say. "My whole stomach is full of butterflies." Even if you're nervous, show up for every standardized test you have to take. In Chapter 6, you'll learn great ways to relax during a standardized test. Then the butterflies will fly away!

4. *Choose your seat carefully.*
Stay away from people who will distract you. Sit close to people who want to do well, as you do.

5. *Read the directions all the way through.*
Say the directions in your own words to make sure you know what you have to do.

6. *Use your time well.*
Spend the most time on the questions that count the most. Spend the least time on the questions that count the least. Pace yourself so you keep on working steadily.

7. *Do your best.*
You might get upset during a standardized test and want to storm out of the room. But stay and finish the test. These tests usually get easier as you go along, because you get into a routine and set up a rhythm.

8. *Be positive.*
Don't beat yourself up if your score isn't what you expected. You'll do better next time.

don't stress

Travon has trouble in school because none of the letters, numbers, or "+" and "-" signs make any sense. By third grade, Travon could only recognize a few words and wrote like a first grader. He repeated third grade to give him time to "catch up." He didn't. He does not do well on standardized tests.

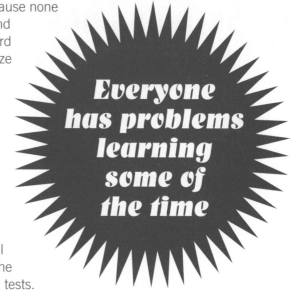

Everyone has problems learning some of the time

Nicole has too much energy. She interrupts the teacher. She's a friendly, well-meaning kid, so her teachers don't get too angry. But she isn't sitting still long enough to learn anything. She does not do well on standardized tests.

Both Travon and Nicole have a **learning disability**. A learning disability affects someone's ability to interpret what they see and hear or to link the information from different parts of the brain. Nearly four million school-age children have learning disabilities. No one is sure what causes a learning disability.

Everyone has problems learning some of the time. But if you find that you have trouble learning nearly all the time, you may have a learning disability. If you suspect that you have a learning disability, first speak with your parent or guardian. Then ask the school to test you for a learning disability.

People with a learning disability can learn. They can do well on standardized tests, too. But they need special help. If you do have a learning disability, you may be given special help for free. By law, public schools must provide special programs.

speak up!

Always talk to an expert if you think that you have a learning disability.

CHAPTER

3

A Few Weeks

Before

Any Standardized Test...

"Football tryouts are in a month," Coach Orobono tells the team. Liam nods. "I have four weeks to get ready," Liam thinks. "This will be a piece of cake. I know I'll make the team."

The month goes by fast. "Let's practice," says his friend Scott. Liam replies, "I want to play with my new puppy, Peanuts. Besides, I know all the football plays."

Suddenly it's the day of the tryouts. "Uh oh," Liam thinks. "I'm not ready at all. I don't remember some of the plays. I wish I had asked Scott to help me." Liam tries out. He doesn't get a place on the team.

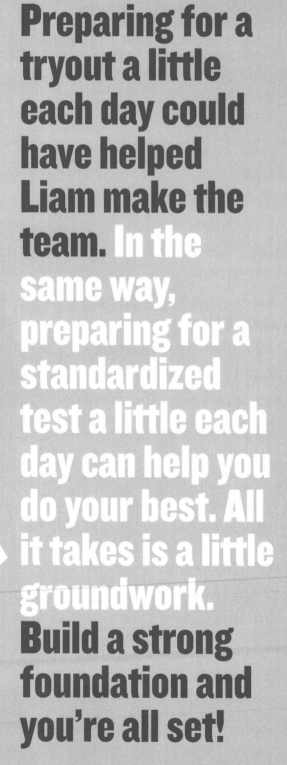

Preparing for a tryout a little each day could have helped Liam make the team. In the same way, preparing for a standardized test a little each day can help you do your best. All it takes is a little groundwork. Build a strong foundation and you're all set!

When the Standardized Test is Announced...

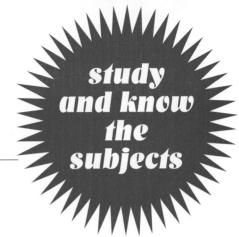

study and know the subjects

First, write the date of the standardized test in your assignment book. Write the time and place, too, if the teacher announces them. You learned how to keep an assignment book in Chapter 2.

Then find out what kind of standardized test you'll be taking. Here are some things to listen for:

* ***What is the name of the test?***
* ***Have you taken this test before?*** If you did, when?
* ***How long is the test?*** Is it half a day? A full day? Or something different?
* ***What subjects will be tested?*** Math? Language Arts? Social Studies? Science?
* ***Will there be a writing section?***
* ***Are the questions multiple-choice?*** Are there any short-answer questions?
* ***Is there an essay?***

Your teacher will probably give the class this information. If the teacher does not, raise your hand and ask.

Catch Up on Any Missing Work

In first grade, you learned how to add single digits. You learned $3 + 3 = 6$. In second grade, you learned how to add double digits. You learned $33 + 41 = 74$. In third grade, you learned more complex math. That's because ***learning builds on learning***. That's why it's important to catch up on any work you missed.

To prepare for any standardized test, catch up on any work you missed. You might have been out of class because of illness, or perhaps you missed class because of a music lesson or speech therapy. No matter what the reason, *you* are responsible for making up all the work you missed. Don't say, "I was not in class. It's not my fault." Take control of your learning. Then you are taking control of your future.

Take Practice Standardized Tests

Remember: Standardized tests are different from regular classroom tests. They have very strict time limits. They have a set format. You must do exactly what you are asked to do. They are usually graded by machine, not your teacher. Standardized tests count for a lot, too. That's why standardized tests are often called "high-stakes" tests.

USE THIS FOUR-STEP PROCESS TO PREPARE FOR A STANDARDIZED TEST A FEW MONTHS OR WEEKS BEFORE THE TEST:

STEP #1
Review all your class notes and past tests.

STEP #2 *Attend all review sessions your teacher holds.*

STEP #3
Learn the format of the test.

STEP #4
Take practice standardized tests. You can often get these on the Web. Your teacher may give you some old tests, too.

**BEFORE YOU STUDY, ARRANGE THE MATERIAL IN ORDER.
HERE ARE TWO METHODS YOU CAN USE:**

ORDER OF IMPORTANCE	ORDER OF DIFFICULTY
Material I *must* learn	*Most* difficult
Material I *should* learn	*Somewhat* difficult
Material I *may need* to learn	*Easy*

repetition helps you remember !

Go over and over the material.
  ✳ Make flashcards.
    ✳ Make summary sheets.
      ✳ Write practice test questions.
       ✳ Teach the material to someone else.
       ✳ Pause often to test yourself.

Also, break your study time into short and long blocks. Use the long blocks to review big ideas. Use the short blocks of time to memorize facts, review those facts, and test yourself.

Below is a sample standardized test. Take it now.

Practice Standardized Reading Test

DIRECTIONS: This part of the test contains a reading passage and five questions. *Read the passage closely and carefully. Then choose the best answer from the four choices. Bubble in the answer of the correct choice.* You have 20 minutes to complete this part of the test.

Responsibilities of Citizens

Citizens of the United States can participate in their government. This process ensures that power will always remain where it belongs—with the people. People who think our obligations are not important are wrong.

The most important obligation citizens have is the right to vote. By voting, the people have a voice in the government. The voters decide who will represent them in the government. Before voting in an election, each citizen should be well informed about the issues and candidates. After voting, citizens should read the newspapers and watch the news to see which candidate won.

The government may call upon citizens to serve on a jury. The members of the jury need to decide the case in as fair a way as they can.

Every person is expected to obey the laws of the community, state, and country in which he or she lives. This helps all Americans to respect the rights of others. All persons living in the United States are expected to pay their income taxes and other taxes honestly and on time.

1. *How many duties do citizens have?*
   Ⓐ one
   Ⓑ two
   Ⓒ four
   Ⓓ ten

2. **Which of the following sentences expresses an opinion?**
Ⓐ People who think our obligations are not important are wrong.
Ⓑ Citizens of the United States can participate in their government.
Ⓒ The government may call upon citizens to serve on a jury.
Ⓓ The voters decide who will represent them in the government.

3. **Read this sentence from the passage:**
The most important obligation citizens have is the right to vote.

Below are four definitions of "right." Which one most likely means the same as the word "right" as it is used in this sentence?
Ⓐ correct
Ⓑ ability
Ⓒ not left
Ⓓ job

4. **What should voters do before any election?**
Ⓐ Serve on a jury and think carefully about the case.
Ⓑ Pay their income taxes and other taxes.
Ⓒ Find out about the candidates' beliefs.
Ⓓ Don't read newspapers or watch television.

5. **Why do you think the author described voting first in the passage?**
Ⓐ It is the most important responsibility.
Ⓑ It is hard to do.
Ⓒ Not everyone can vote.
Ⓓ Very few people vote.

Scoring Sheet

1.	Ⓐ	Ⓑ	Ⓒ	Ⓓ
2.	Ⓐ	Ⓑ	Ⓒ	Ⓓ
3.	Ⓐ	Ⓑ	Ⓒ	Ⓓ
4.	Ⓐ	Ⓑ	Ⓒ	Ⓓ
5.	Ⓐ	Ⓑ	Ⓒ	Ⓓ

ANSWERS
1.C, 2. A, 3. B, 4. C, 5. A

If you want to hit a home run... **practice!** *If you want to swim well...* **practice!** *If you want to make the perfect grilled cheese sandwich...practice! If you want to do well on standardized tests...* (hint...it means **prepare**...) **practice!**

GO OVER YOUR ANSWERS ON THIS PRACTICE TEST.
See what answers you got right. See what parts you didn't understand. Where did you make a mistake? Maybe you didn't know the meaning of a word. Maybe you didn't understand a sentence. Maybe you read too fast and skipped an important fact. *Not to worry: Practice to the rescue!*

Take the **Practice Standardized Reading Test** *again.*
Use the methods that worked well the first time.

it does make perfect!

No Excuses!

Cassandra means to take practice standardized tests. She really does. The teacher gives the class a lot of them. It's just that she keeps putting it off. By the time she's finally ready to sit down, there's no time.

Zane starts to take a practice standardized test every day. Then he takes a break, but he can't get back to work after his break. The rest of the night, he plays video games.

Blake always has something fun to do. Monday she's invited to a party. Tuesday she goes shopping. Wednesday is an emergency Student Council meeting. Thursday is play tryouts. The practice standardized tests just don't get done.

WHAT EXCUSES DO YOU MAKE NOT TO TAKE PRACTICE STANDARDIZED TESTS?
Take this quiz to see.
Check off the excuses that you have used.

1. *I don't have a study schedule.*

2. *It's (baseball, soccer, juggling, spoon-on-nose, etc.) season.*

3. *I just got a new (puppy, kitten, iguana, dinosaur, etc.).*

4. *I don't have any practice standardized tests. I think I lost them.*

5. *I have too many practice standardized tests. My teacher gives us one every day! The pile of tests scares me.*

6. *Time seems to slip away.*

7. *Extracurricular activities are more fun.*

8. *I don't understand the practice standardized test.*

9. *I keep falling asleep when I take a practice standardized test.*

10. *The passages on practice standardized tests are boring.*

TAKING A PRACTICE STANDARDIZED TEST TAKES LESS TIME THAN MAKING EXCUSES!

Here's how to take care of each excuse:

1. *Make a study schedule.* You learned how in Chapter 2.

2. Sports are important, but school comes first. *Try to balance sports and school.* If you can't, play sports with some friends rather than on a formal team.

3. *Play with your pet during your five-minute study break.*

4. *Talk to your teacher and get copies of the practice standardized tests you lost.*

5. *Pick a test, any test.* Since they are standard, it doesn't make a difference!

6. *Get an egg timer.* Set the timer. When it rings, it's time to take a practice standardized test.

7. Extracurricular activities are fun, but they have to be balanced with your schoolwork. *Be sure to have enough time to study.* Then you will do your best.

8. *Get extra help.*

9. *Start earlier in the day.* Don't work in bed. Instead, complete the test in a chair at a desk.

10. *Pretend you are a detective solving a mystery.* Read the test questions first. Then read the passage. Look for the facts you need to find to answer each question.

If you get bored, do another part of the test. Do the math part instead of the reading questions. Read instead of doing math problems. Or, write the essay.

CHAPTER 4

Kai walks into the standardized test feeling confident. He's studied, taken practice tests, and gone to extra help. He's eaten a good breakfast, too. Kai knows how to prepare for standardized tests. He also knows how to take standardized tests. This chapter will help *you* do your best the day of any standardized test.

On the Day of Any Standardized Test...

Carpenters say "measure twice, cut once." That's because they know that planning ahead pays off in the end. By planning, carpenters build better houses. They waste less time and wood, too. In the same way, good test takers plan ahead. They know that planning ahead helps them do their best on all standardized tests. It helps them relax, too, so they don't feel as nervous. *Here are some ways to plan ahead for success on the day of the standardized test:*

1. *Know the test rules.*

For example, you may not be allowed to bring your cell phone, backpack, or snack. You may have to leave your jacket outside, too. Plan ahead by knowing what you can and can't bring with you. Then just bring the things you're allowed to bring.

2. *Carry supplies.*

Be sure to have pens, pencils, and your calculator. Bring extra batteries for your calculator. Wear a watch so you can keep track of the time.

3. *Bring identification.*

You won't need a school ID for a class test, of course. Your teacher knows who you are. But for a standardized test, you may need one. You may need a test letter or some other ticket for admission, too. Be sure to check ahead so you know if you need an ID. Then, be sure to have the proof with you on the day of the standardized test.

4. *Arrive early.*

Paige gets lost everywhere! But Paige is smart. The day before a standardized test, she takes a practice trip to the test site. Then she can relax the day of the test because she knows where she is going. She knows she won't be late.

leave early

Most of the standardized tests you take will be in your school—but not all of them. Some standardized tests will be given at other schools, such as the district high school. You may also take standardized tests at test centers. So make sure you know how to get to the test center. Ask a parent to drive you a few days early so you both know how to get there. If you take a subway or bus, practice a few days before. If you walk or ride your bike, take a practice trip. Leave yourself at least 15 minutes to spare. For example, if the test starts at 8:00, you should be there by 7:45.

Follow the Directions

You may have only one hour to do the standardized test. Or, you may have a whole day. No matter how much time you have, it won't seem like enough. So you want to start the test right away. Don't! Instead, read the directions. Then read them again. Also listen carefully to any directions the teacher gives. Make sure you understand all the directions before you make a mark on the test.

After you read the directions, follow them *exactly*. Some students do poorly on standardized tests because they don't follow the directions. For instance, they write their answers on the test rather than on the separate answer sheet. Or they write in pen rather than pencil.

Set Up a Test Strategy

1. Preview the test.

You've read the directions. Now you can start the test, right? Wrong! Instead, skim the test to see what's on it. You might find just what you expected, but there might be some surprises. Knowing what's on the test helps you move on to the next planning step.

2. Decide what to do first.

THERE ARE SEVERAL DIFFERENT WAYS TO TAKE A STANDARDIZED TEST. HERE ARE SOME GOOD PLANS:

METHOD #1

Work from the first question to the last question. Answer every question. Put a question mark next to any questions you're not sure you answered correctly. If you have time, go back to these questions later. Check your answers.

METHOD #2

Answer all the easy questions first. Then go back and answer the harder questions. For example, answer the easy multiple-choice questions first. Put a check mark next to the ones you find difficult. Then, go back and answer the difficult questions. Or, if you find writing easier than answering multiple-choice test items, write the essay first. Then, do the multiple-choice questions.

METHOD #3

This is the opposite of Method #2. Here, answer all the hard questions first. Next, go back and answer the easier questions. For example, if you find the essay hard, write it first. As a result, you'll have the hardest part of the test out of the way. Then answer the part you find easy: the multiple-choice questions.

Most people like Plan #1 and Plan #2 the best. But you should choose the plan that works best for you on each standardized test.

3. *Plan your time.*

You're *still* not ready to start! Now, figure out how much time you should spend on each part of the standardized test. For example, if you have 100 multiple-choice questions and 100 minutes, spend one minute on each question. What should you do if you can't answer a question after one minute? Go on to the next question! You'll earn a higher score if you keep working. That's because you'll get more right answers.

What should you do if the questions don't divide so neatly? Say you have one hour for the standardized test. You have an essay that counts 60 points and multiple-choice questions that count 40 points. Spend the most time on the part that counts the most. On this standardized test, it's the essay. That's where you should spend more time.

The items on standardized tests are often arranged from easiest to harder. Therefore, you have to plan your time carefully. Spend less time on the first questions because they are easier. Spend more time on the last questions because they are harder.

4. *Decide if you should guess.*

What happens if you get stumped on a question? If you get points taken off for guessing, don't guess wildly. First, try to cross out some choices. If you get down to two choices, you have a 50 percent chance of being correct. Then it pays to guess.

If you don't get points taken off for guessing, fill in every answer. Don't leave any blank.

ALL THIS PLANNING SHOULDN'T TAKE YOU A LOT OF TIME. SET ASIDE ABOUT FIVE MINUTES TO PLAN.

Keep Your Cool

PLANNING AHEAD AND HAVING A TEST STRATEGY WILL HELP REDUCE TEST JITTERS.

But if you still feel yourself getting tense, try these ideas:

1. *Look over your work.* Seeing a lot of correct answers will help you calm down.
2. *Imagine yourself doing well.* Imagine answering all the questions easily.
3. *Pause for a minute or two.* Take three deep breaths.
4. *Be positive.* Think about all you know, not everything you don't know.

DEALING WITH TEST JITTERS IS COVERED IN DETAIL IN CHAPTER 6.

Take these sample standardized tests now.
Use the skills that you have learned so far.
Be sure to follow the directions, set up a test strategy,
and keep your cool.

Practice Standardized Math Test

DIRECTIONS: *Answer all questions from this part.* Each correct answer will receive 2 credits. No partial credit will be allowed. You have 15 minutes to complete this part of the test.

1. *Which of these is the number 3,002,011?*
   Ⓐ three thousand, two hundred, eleven
   Ⓑ three million, two hundred, eleven
   Ⓒ three million, two thousand, eleven
   Ⓓ three billion, two million, eleven

2. *Which of the numbers below has the greatest value?*
   Ⓐ 16.3
   Ⓑ 0.16
   Ⓒ 3.16
   Ⓓ 7.91

3. *Which fraction represents the largest part of a whole?*
   Ⓐ 1/2
   Ⓑ 1/9
   Ⓒ 1/4
   Ⓓ 1/10

4. *What is 723, 823 rounded to the nearest hundred?*
   Ⓐ 800,000
   Ⓑ 723,800
   Ⓒ 723,820
   Ⓓ 723,000

5. **What is the next number in this pattern?**

   12, 9, 6, 3, 0, ___

   Ⓐ 2

   Ⓑ 1

   Ⓒ -6

   Ⓓ -3

6. **There are 61 cases of water for field day. If there are 24 bottles of water in each case, how many bottles of water are there?**

   Ⓐ 85

   Ⓑ 1,446

   Ⓒ 1,464

   Ⓓ 35,136

7. **Which is a prime number?**

   Ⓐ 6

   Ⓑ 3

   Ⓒ 9

   Ⓓ 16

8. **What is the value of x in this equation?**

   185 - x = 148

   Ⓐ 73

   Ⓑ 37

   Ⓒ 91

   Ⓓ 333

9. **Jacqui walked 64 miles in 16 days. She walked the same amount each day. How many miles did she walk each day?**

   Ⓐ 4

   Ⓑ 8

   Ⓒ 2

   Ⓓ 1

10. **What is the value of the expression below?**

    (15 + 9) - (5 x 3)

    Ⓐ 0

    Ⓑ 6

    Ⓒ 7

    Ⓓ 9

ANSWERS

1.C, **2.** A, **3.** A, **4.** B, **5.** D,
6.C, **7.** B, **8.** B, **9.** A, **10.** D

Practice Standardized History/Social Studies Test

DIRECTIONS: This part of the test has a map, timeline, and five questions. *Study the visuals. Then choose the best answer from the four choices.* Bubble in the answer of the correct choice. You have 15 minutes to complete this part of the test.

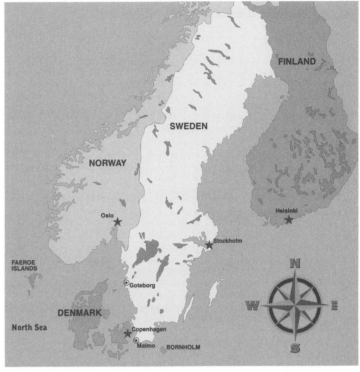

Source: United Nations Cyberschoolbus (cyberschoolbus.un.org)

1. ***This map shows all the following countries BUT***
   - Ⓐ Norway
   - Ⓑ Sweden
   - Ⓒ India
   - Ⓓ Finland

2. ***What is off the west coast of Denmark?***
   - Ⓐ Poland
   - Ⓑ Germany
   - Ⓒ the Baltic Sea
   - Ⓓ the North Sea

3. ***Copenhagen is located closest to***
   - Ⓐ Sweden
   - Ⓑ Finland
   - Ⓒ Faeroe Islands
   - Ⓓ Norway

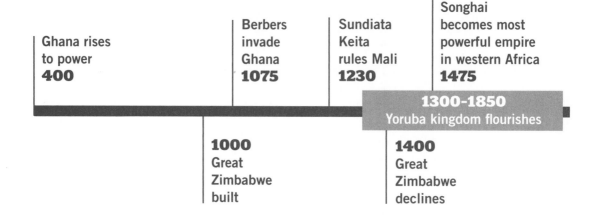

Ghana rises to power **400**		Berbers invade Ghana **1075**	Sundiata Keita rules Mali **1230**	Songhai becomes most powerful empire in western Africa **1475**

1300–1850
Yoruba kingdom flourishes

1000 Great Zimbabwe built

1400 Great Zimbabwe declines

4. ***When did the kingdom of Songhai flourish?***
Ⓐ after the Yoruba kingdom
Ⓑ after Ghana rose to power
Ⓒ while the Berbers invaded Ghana
Ⓓ before Great Zimbabwe was built

5. ***For about how many years did Great Zimbabwe exist?***
Ⓐ 100
Ⓑ 200
Ⓒ 400
Ⓓ 600

Scoring Sheet

1. Ⓐ Ⓑ Ⓒ Ⓓ
2. Ⓐ Ⓑ Ⓒ Ⓓ
3. Ⓐ Ⓑ Ⓒ Ⓓ
4. Ⓐ Ⓑ Ⓒ Ⓓ
5. Ⓐ Ⓑ Ⓒ Ⓓ

ANSWERS
1.C, 2. D, 3. A, 4. B, 5. C

Taking practice standardized tests helps you prepare in many ways. These tests help you learn the types of questions you will have to answer. This gets you ready for the big day! They help you build speed and confidence, too.

CHAPTER 4: **On The Day of Any Standardized Test**

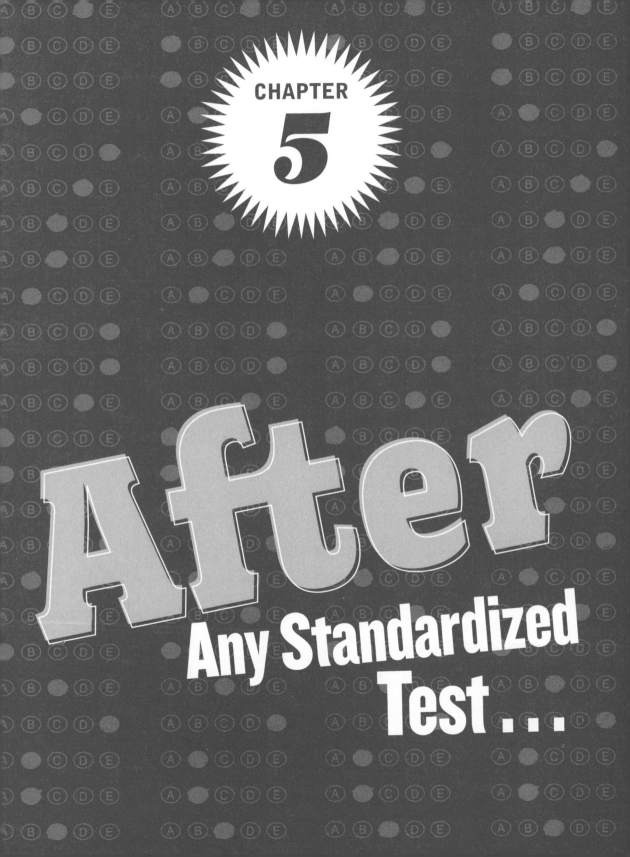

Each standardized test you take helps you do better on the next test— if you think about the test. That's because test taking is a skill. And like any skill, it can be learned.

it's not luck!

Study Your Answers

WHICH STUDENT IS GETTING THE MOST LEARNING FROM A STANDARDIZED TEST?

Matt gets back his PSAT. He knows the lowest score is 20 and the top score is 80. He got a 75. Happily, he throws the test into his notebook. He says to himself, "Whoopee!"

Gabriel gets back his PSAT. He knows the lowest score is 20 and the top score is 80. He got a 32 on the multiple-choice verbal portion. He's furious! He crumples the test and tosses it on the floor.

Jade gets back her PSAT writing test. She did not do well. She feels a little teary, but she looks at the test, anyway. She says to herself, "Let me see what I can learn from this. Then I can do better next time."

Matt got a top score, but he can still learn from the test. He can see what study methods helped him the most and use this knowledge the next time he studies. Then, he could study more easily. *Gabriel is missing a good chance to assess his performance.* Maybe he just made a careless error. For example, he might understand the material, but have marked all the answers in the wrong places on the answer sheet. Next time, he would be more careful. *Jade is getting the most learning from the test.* She knows that tests are like maps. They help you get where you want to go in life.

Most of the time, you will not get a standardized test back. Then you can't go over your answers as carefully as you can with the test in front of you. You have to remember the questions you missed and the questions you got correct. You *do* get the PSAT and SAT back. Then you can go over these tests.

The PSAT is the practice test for the SAT. The PSAT helps you get ready for the SAT. The SAT is the test you take to help you get into the college you want. Some kids take the PSAT in 5th or 6th grade. Most kids take the PSAT in middle school. The PSAT is important for other reasons, too. The PSAT is used to give out scholarships. It is also used to help you get into special summer programs.

LIKE THE SAT, THE PSAT HAS THREE PARTS:

✶ *Critical Reading:* Two 25-minute parts. They are sentence completion, paragraphs, and reading comprehension.

✶ *Math:* Two 25-minute parts. They are multiple-choice questions and short answers. The subjects are geometry, algebra I, data interpretation, and logic.

✶ *Writing Skills:* One 30-minute part containing sentence error questions, sentence improvement questions, and paragraph improvement questions. The PSAT Writing Skills section does *not* include an essay. However, you will have to write an essay for the SAT.

If you do get a standardized test back, study it carefully. See what you did right. See what you didn't understand. Figure out what caused your errors. Then you'll know what to do differently on the next test. **If you don't get the test back, think about the questions.** You'll remember some of them. Think about how you felt when you took the test. Did you panic? *In both cases, use a checklist like the one below.*

Always correct every question that you missed. Then you know that you really understand the material.

Use a Checklist

1. *What questions did I get right?*
   What skills helped me answer them correctly?

2. *Which questions did I misread?*
   What words confused me?
   How can I learn these words?

3. *Did I misunderstand some ideas?*
   If so, which ones? Should I go for extra help?

4. *Where did I make careless mistakes?*
   What caused these mistakes? Should I read more slowly and carefully next time?

5. *Did I run out of time?*
   If so, how can I pace myself better next time?

6. *Was the scorer able to read my handwriting?* Should I print next time?

7. *Did I study the wrong material?* Should I have studied more? Should I have studied differently?

8. *Did I second-guess myself?*
   (This happens when you get the answer right, but then change it.) If so, how can I stop doing this?

9. *Did I guess too much?* What can I do to increase my chances of guessing correctly?

10. *What was my biggest error?*
    What caused me to make this error?

11. *Is there a pattern of mistakes?*
    This shows I didn't understand some big ideas. Should I go for extra help and reread my textbook and notes?

12. *Did I panic?* If so, how can I control test panic next time?

Talk With Your Teacher

Your teacher can help you look over your test and focus your studying. That way, you'll do better next time. Teachers can also help you get some distance from the test. This means that you won't be as upset if you didn't do as well as you expected. You'll feel better when you have some specific ways to improve.

Some standardized tests have been graded wrong. That's another reason to go over your test if you get it back. Check your answers to make sure that each answer is graded correctly. Check that the points are totaled correctly. If you find a problem, go over it with a parent. Then you and your parent can decide what to do.

Try it Again!

If you fall off a horse, you get right back on. Back in the saddle, partner! Take this language arts test. It follows a standardized test format. Use the ideas you have learned from the book, especially this chapter, as you take the test.

don't be upset

Go for Extra Help

Emma has trouble on standardized tests. The tests are so long! The questions don't come straight from the textbook, either. "What can I do?" Emma asks. "I know that standardized tests are very important." Then there's Leo. He is already going for extra help, but it's not helping him do better on standardized tests. ***What can Emma and Leo do?***

Emma can go for extra help. She should tell the tutor that she is finding standardized tests difficult. The tutor can concentrate on helping Emma prepare for standardized tests. The tutor can give Emma practice tests, for instance. Leo can try another form of extra help. Maybe he could attend the school resource room. Perhaps he could ask his family or friends for help. Often, other teachers in the school give extra help as well.

Practice Standardized English/Language Arts Test

DIRECTIONS: *Answer all questions from this part.* Each correct answer will receive 2 credits. No partial credit will be allowed. Write your answers on the scoring sheet. You have 30 minutes to complete this part of the test.

The Lion and the Mouse

A Lion was awakened from sleep by a Mouse running over his face. Rising up angrily, the Lion caught the Mouse and was about to kill him. The Mouse piteously entreated, saying: "If you would only spare my life, I would be sure to repay your kindness." The Lion laughed and let him go.

Soon after, some hunters caught the Lion and bound him by strong ropes to the ground. The Mouse, recognizing the Lion's roar, came and gnawed the rope with his teeth and set him free, exclaiming: "You ridiculed the idea of my ever being able to help you, expecting to receive from me any repayment of your favor. Now you know that it is possible for even a Mouse to help a Lion."

Elephants

The largest mammals on earth today are elephants. They are huge even from birth: Elephant calves weigh around 265 pounds! The largest elephant ever recorded was caught in 1974. It was male and weighed 26,400 pounds. The smallest elephants, about the size of a calf or a large pig, were a prehistoric variety that lived on the island of Crete. An elephant may live as long as 70 years, sometimes longer. African elephants are distinguished from Asians in several ways. The most noticeable difference is the ears. Africans' ears are much larger and are shaped like the continent of their origin. The African elephant is typically larger than the Asian and has a concave back. Both males and females have external tusks and are usually less hairy than their Asian cousins. The elephant is now a protected animal. As a result, keeping one as a pet is prohibited around the world.

1. *The first passage is* **best** *described as a*
ⓐ fairy tale from long ago.
ⓑ modern-day science fiction story.
ⓒ story from another country.
ⓓ fable that teaches readers a lesson.

2. *The second passage is* **best** *described as*
ⓐ a myth that explains how something began.
ⓑ an editorial that expresses the writer's opinion.
ⓒ an essay that provides factual information.
ⓓ an excerpt from a traveler's journal.

3. *Read this sentence from "The Lion and the Mouse."*

The Mouse piteously entreated, saying: "If you would only spare my life, I would be sure to repay your kindness."

Which word is a **synonym** *for* **entreated?**
ⓐ begged
ⓑ asked
ⓒ demanded
ⓓ walked

4. *The Lion in "The Lion and the Mouse" laughs at the Mouse because the Lion*
ⓐ didn't expect the Mouse to be able to talk.
ⓑ didn't think the Mouse would ever be able to help him.
ⓒ believed the Mouse was very adorable.
ⓓ was tickled when the Mouse ran over his face.

5. *What is the theme of "The Lion and the Mouse"?*
ⓐ Happy is the person who learns from the misfortunes of others.
ⓑ All people and animals control their own fate.
ⓒ No act of kindness, no matter how small, is ever wasted.
ⓓ Those who seek to please everybody please nobody.

6. **African and Asian elephants are different in all the following ways BUT**
Ⓐ length of life span
Ⓑ ear size and shape
Ⓒ size and weight
Ⓓ back shape

7. **From reading "Elephants," you can conclude that**
Ⓐ elephants are a friendly species and make good pets.
Ⓑ scientists have studied elephants and know a lot about them.
Ⓒ all elephants are about the same size, shape, and weight.
Ⓓ elephants are found all over the world, especially in Asia.

8. **Read this sentence from "Elephants."**

The elephant is now a protected animal. As a result, keeping one as a pet is prohibited around the world.

Which word is an antonym for prohibited?
Ⓐ encouraged
Ⓑ allowed
Ⓒ forbidden
Ⓓ tolerated

9. **From the information in "Elephants," you can most logically infer that**
Ⓐ elephants were once a good food source.
Ⓑ many people want to keep elephants as pets.
Ⓒ people still use elephants as transportation.
Ⓓ all the small elephants have died out.

10. **These passages were most likely paired because they both**
Ⓐ tell about elephants.
Ⓑ come from other countries.
Ⓒ support kindness to animals.
Ⓓ have the same author.

SCORE YOUR TEST. Then use the checklist in this chapter to go over your test. Find your "trouble spots." Maybe you read too fast. Perhaps you have to learn more vocabulary. Develop ways to fix your problems, using the methods in this book.

Scoring Sheet

1. Ⓐ Ⓑ Ⓒ Ⓓ
2. Ⓐ Ⓑ Ⓒ Ⓓ
3. Ⓐ Ⓑ Ⓒ Ⓓ
4. Ⓐ Ⓑ Ⓒ Ⓓ
5. Ⓐ Ⓑ Ⓒ Ⓓ
6. Ⓐ Ⓑ Ⓒ Ⓓ
7. Ⓐ Ⓑ Ⓒ Ⓓ
8. Ⓐ Ⓑ Ⓒ Ⓓ
9. Ⓐ Ⓑ Ⓒ Ⓓ
10. Ⓐ Ⓑ Ⓒ Ⓓ

ANSWERS
1.D, 2. C, 3. A, 4. B, 5. C, 6. A, 7. B, 8. C, 9. D, 10. A

CHAPTER 5: **After Any Standardized Test**

CHAPTER
6

Deal with Test
Worry

"I get butterflies in my stomach before a standardized test," Rashina says. D'Shaun calls that tense feeling in his stomach "standardized test jitters." Blake and Sophie get sweaty hands and feel like they can't sit still when they see a standardized test being handed out. How about you?

How do standardized tests make *you* feel?

Most students get a little nervous before a standardized test. That's natural – and it's not always a bad thing! That's because a minor case of the nerves can help you do better. Being a little tense helps you stay sharp and focus your attention.

But being too nervous can prevent you from doing your best. Fortunately, there are good ways to calm down before a standardized test. They're pretty easy, too. Best of all, they work great. You learned a little bit about dealing with test worry in Chapter 4. Let's focus on it in this chapter.

Deal with Your Own Fears

you can calm yourself down

Some pressure comes from yourself. This usually happens when you make the test seem more important than it is. Standardized test *do* matter, that's true. But remember: Standardized tests give only part of the picture of who you are. Reduce your fear by saying to yourself, "I can make myself nervous. I can make myself calmer. Which way do I want to feel?" Of course, you want to feel calmer.

TRY THESE IDEAS:

✴ *Before the test, take some deep breaths.*
Slowly take a breath through your nose. Then breathe out your mouth. Do this three times. Be very quiet so you don't disturb your neighbors.

✴ *Before the test, think of a restful scene.*
It might be a day at the beach or lake. It might be a camping trip with family and friends. Picture it in your mind to remember how it looks. Think about the clear blue sky dotted with fluffy white clouds at the ocean. Recall the sounds you heard. Can you hear the crash of the waves? The cawing of the seagulls? Remember the smell of the salty ocean air and the coconut suntan oil. Spend about a minute at your restful place. Then start the test.

You can use these calming methods during a standardized test as well. If you feel the panic rising, pause for a second. Take some deep breaths. Think about your restful place for a minute. Remember: You can make yourself upset. Just as easily, you can calm yourself down.

A memory lapse is perfectly normal, so don't let it throw you into a panic. If you block on answering a question, leave it for awhile and return to it later.

Some pressure comes from friends. Often, this happens when friends brag, "Oh, I don't review practice tests at all and I earned the best score in the school on the Terra Nova." Don't believe them! They're studying when you don't see them. But they make you feel more nervous because you wonder, "How can they have it so easy? Why do they feel so calm? What are they doing that I'm not?" Ignore what these friends say.

Second, stay away from friends who make you feel more nervous. You know who these people are. They say things like, "This test will be really hard. We're going to do poorly." Or "My stomach really hurts. I bet you feel just as sick because of the standardized test coming up."

Finally, during a standardized test, you may see other students finishing before you do. Ignore them. Take your time and you'll do much better on the test.

* **Use all your time.**
  Even if you finish early, don't leave.
* **Check your work.**
* **Then check it again!**

Most of all: Compare yourself to *you*. Don't compare yourself to anyone else.

Deal with Pressure

From Friends

From Parents

Parents can add to the pressure, too. They want you to do well. They don't want to add to your nervousness, but sometimes, their help makes you feel even more tense. How can you cope with this?

Remember that your family members went to school and took standardized tests, too. They might still take standardized tests for their jobs. Accountants have to earn a good score on a standardized test called the "CPA Exam." Doctors and nurses have to pass state standardized exams before they can practice. Even teachers have to take standardized tests! Many states make teachers earn a good score on a standardized test called the "Praxis Exam." So, they've been in your shoes.

What should you do if parents give you advice about taking standardized tests? Listen! Then ask them for ways that they deal with test panic. Last, recognize that your parents are proud of you. They know you want to do well. Then do your very best.

Prepare Thoroughly

One of the best ways to feel less nervous is to study. That's just common sense. But a lot of students try to "wing it." They don't review practice tests at home. Sometimes they think that listening in class is enough. They don't make time to study. That's because they don't understand how being well prepared for a standardized test really helps reduce test panic.

You know that studying and going over old exams helps you relax. You'll have less panic if you are sure you know the material. But full preparation means more than just knowing the test material. It's also very important to prepare your mind and body for a test.

TRY THESE IDEAS:

1. *Take practice tests.*
You've heard it over and over in this book. Duck your head because here it comes again: Take practice standardized tests! Taking practice tests is a great way to reduce test anxiety. You learned that your teacher might give you some practice tests. You can make up your own test questions, too. Use your textbook and notes to get the topics.

2. *Eat breakfast.*
Fewer butterflies will fly around your stomach if it has some food in it. If you're really too nervous to eat before you leave the house, grab some fruit to eat on the bus. Never take a standardized test on an empty stomach.

3. *Get enough sleep.*
Not just the night before the test, either! Get into the habit of sleeping at least eight hours a night. Being well-rested helps hold panic off.

4. *Lay out your clothes and supplies the night before.*
You'll feel calmer if you're not rushing around in the morning.

5. *Arrive early at the test site.*
Few things make people lose their cool as much as dashing in late.

6. *Be seated at your desk and ready to take the test.*
Then you can do some relaxation exercises.

Work Carefully

Remember the turtle and the hare? The hare started off fast but lost steam halfway through the race. The turtle plodded along at a steady pace. The turtle won. The moral of the story is: "Slow and steady wins the race."

This is true when it comes to tests as well. Work at a smooth, steady pace. Then you'll feel less nervous because you will see progress. You'll know you're getting through the test.

THESE TIPS CAN HELP YOU KEEP UP THE PACE:

* *Make certain that you fully understand the test directions before you try to solve any math problems or answer any questions.*

* *Plan how you will use your time during the standardized test.*
   Quickly look over the entire test and divide up your available time as appropriate to the number and type of questions that you find. You'll feel more relaxed once you have a plan.

* *Read each question carefully and completely before you mark your answer.*

* *Reread the test questions if you get confused.*

do your *best*

Take the Long View

You might do poorly on a standardized test like the Iowa Tests of Basic Skills this year. Don't throw up your hands in despair. That will just make you feel more tense the next time you take the test.

Instead, look ahead. Think about all the standardized tests you take. Promise yourself to learn from your mistakes. Always try your best. If you do, you'll feel a lot less test panic.

ahead!

CHAPTER 6: Deal With Test Worry

CHAPTER 7

Standardized tests are similar to classroom tests in many ways. Like classroom tests, standardized tests have different formats. Some are multiple-choice, others are short-answer, and still others are essay. Many standardized tests have all three types of questions—just like classroom tests. That's why you have to know all the different formats. In this chapter, you'll learn how to do well on standardized tests with multiple-choice questions. Then you can do even better on both classroom and standardized tests.

Multiple-Choice Standardized Tests

Succeed on *All* Multiple-Choice Standardized Test Items

USE THIS THREE-STEP PROCESS AS YOU TACKLE
MULTIPLE-CHOICE ITEMS ON STANDARDIZED TESTS.

STEP #1
Read the question.
Restate difficult questions
in your own words. You
may need to try several
different ways until you
understand the question.

STEP #2
Predict the answers.
Cover the answer choices.
Decide what the correct
answer should be.

STEP #3
Read all the answers
and make your choice.
Look for the answer
that is the best match
for your prediction.
If you can't find it,
rethink the question.
Did you misunderstand
the question?
If so, what part did
you not get?

Sample Question TRY IT NOW:

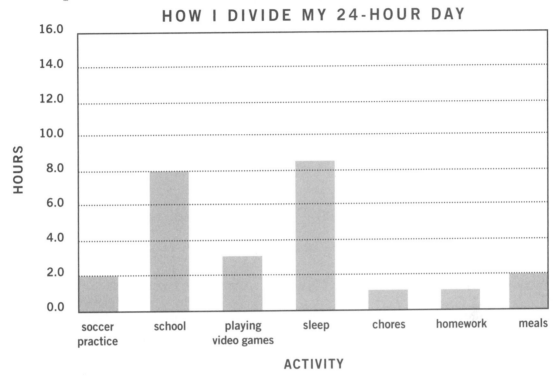

HOW I DIVIDE MY 24-HOUR DAY

This chart shows how Elijah spends an average day.
Which two activities take up the same amount of time every day?

Ⓐ going to school and sleeping
Ⓑ doing chores and eating meals
Ⓒ playing video games and sleeping
Ⓓ eating meals and playing soccer

EXPLANATION: This is a bar graph. ***To read a bar graph, study the title, the labels, and the height of each bar.*** Then read the question and restate it in your own words. The question asks you to find the two things Elijah does that match in time.

ANSWER: *Choice A is wrong* because Elijah spends 8 hours going to school. He spends 8½ hours sleeping. He spends half an hour more sleeping so they are not the same amount of time. ***Choice B is wrong*** because Elijah spends 1 hour doing chores. He spends 2 hours eating meals. He spends half an hour more eating so they are not the same amount of time, either. ***Choice C is wrong*** because Elijah spends 3 hours playing video games. He spends 8½ hours sleeping. He spends six more hours sleeping so they are not the same amount of time. ***Choice D is correct*** because Elijah spends 2 hours eating meals. He spends 2 hours playing soccer. This is the same amount of time.

Hints for Scoring High on Multiple-Choice Standardized Tests

Use these hints to do well on multiple-choice standardized test items.

HINT	DETAIL
1. Circle or underline important words.	This helps you find the central point and get the correct answer.
2. Use process of elimination.	Cross out answers that are silly or clearly off the topic.
3. Read every answer choice.	Even if you're sure that choice Ⓐ is correct, read all the way to the last choice. You may find that it's even better than your original choice.
4. Do the easy questions first.	This helps build confidence.
5. Skip questions you don't know.	You can go back to them if you have enough time. You want to answer as many questions as you can.
6. Watch the *all of the above* choice.	For the answer to be *all of the above*, every part of every choice has to be correct.
7. Use all your time.	If you finish early, recheck your answers.
8. Circle or underline important words.	Be sure to erase all stray marks.

pace yourself!

What was the <u>purpose</u> of <u>both</u> the <u>Magna Carta</u> and the <u>English Bill of Rights</u>?

Which food does the body break down to release energy?
Ⓐ *sugar*
Ⓑ ~~*wood*~~　　　　　　**People don't eat wood!**
Ⓒ *bread*

Which is the best *synonym for <u>revolting</u>?*
Ⓐ *gross*
Ⓑ *turning*　　　　**Choice A is good, but "gross" is slang**
Ⓒ *attractive*　　　**and can also mean "large." Choice D is better.**
Ⓓ *repulsive*

Luca skims the entire test before he starts working.
Then he goes back and answers the questions he knows.

Caitlyn puts a ✓ next to the questions she skips. At the end of the test,
she goes back to these questions. She is always very careful to erase all her ✓ marks.

The US government includes
Ⓐ *a legislative branch.*
Ⓑ *an executive branch.*　　**Choices A, B, and C are all part of**
Ⓒ *a judicial branch.*　　　**the US government.**
Ⓓ *all of the above.*

Paris left a standardized test early. Then she realized a mistake she had made.
She could not go back to fix it.

Standardized tests are graded by machines.
Machines see stray marks as incorrect answers.

Just for Multiple-Choice Standardized Language Arts and Reading Tests

1 *Pace yourself carefully.*
You need enough time to read the passage and to answer the questions. Plan your time. Then work steadily.

2 *First read the entire passage (or both paired passages).*
This helps you get an overview for a general understanding. Don't worry about words you don't know. You'll figure them out later.

3 *Reread the passage(s).*
Pause at sections you find more difficult. Look for the main ideas and key details.

4 *Scan the multiple-choice questions without looking at the answers.*
As you already learned, predict the answer. Then look at the choices and find the closest match.

5 *Find proof in the text.*
Return to the text to find proof for each of your answers. For questions on main ideas and specific details, try to find exact lines. For questions about drawing conclusions and making inferences, find details.

make a plan

Answering Specific Questions

There are different types of multiple-choice questions.
HERE ARE WAYS TO ANSWER THEM.

Main-Idea Questions

Look at the title and the topic sentence.
The **topic sentence** states the main idea of the passage.
The topic sentence will usually be the first sentence in the
passage. All the details in the passage support the topic
sentence and the main idea it states. Below are some
ways a main-idea question can be written.
There are other ways as well.

What is the main event in this story?
What is the author's main idea?

Draw-a-Conclusion and Make-Inference Questions

*Use details from the passage and what you
already know to find unstated information.*
You're making an educated guess. Below are
some ways that draw-a-conclusion and make-
inference questions can be written:

The information in the passage supports the idea that...
The main character learns that...
You can conclude that...
How does the main character feel at the end of the story?

Questions About Defining Unfamiliar Words

Use structural clues and context clues. **Structural clues** are prefixes, suffixes, and roots. Prefixes are a letter or letters at the beginning of a word that change its meaning. Suffixes are a letter or letters at the end of a word that change its meaning. Roots are the base form of the word. **HERE ARE SOME EXAMPLES:**

WORD	PREFIX AND MEANING	ROOT AND MEANING
inequality	in- = not	equal = same
disenchantment	dis- = not	enchant = charm

Context clues are the words and phrases in a sentence that give clues to the meaning of a difficult word. **HERE IS AN EXAMPLE:**

The second grade class had several **precocious** students. One child had *learned to read at age three* and another could do *algebra at age six.*

From the underlined context clues, you can figure out that *precocious* means "showing unusually early development or maturity, especially in mental aptitude."

Make-Prediction Questions

Preview the title, subtitle, and headings. Look at any pictures or other visuals. Use this information to make a logical guess about what will come next in the passage.

SUFFIX AND MEANING	WORD MEANING
-ity = state of being	unfairness, not being equal
-ment = state of being	unhappiness, dissatisfaction

Try what you learned now!

Complete the following sample standardized English/Language Arts test.

TRY TO FOLLOW TEST CONDITIONS:
* *Sit in a quiet room*
* *Turn off the TV and cell phone*
* *Take the test in one sitting*
* *Time yourself*

Practice Standardized English/Language Arts Test

DIRECTIONS: This part of the test has a reading passage and five questions. *Read the passage carefully. Then choose the best answer from the four choices.* Bubble in the answer of the correct choice. You have 20 minutes to complete this part of the test.

The Nebraska Quarter

The Nebraska quarter has a picture of pioneers in a covered wagon. This picture fits the state where major trails to the West began!

Eastern Nebraska used to be part of French Louisiana, which the United States bought in the Louisiana Purchase of 1803. Lewis and Clark explored the region the following year, and Zebulon M. Pike explored it in 1806. Robert Stuart pioneered the Oregon Trail across Nebraska in 1812. The Oregon Trail linked with the California Trail and the Mormon Trail. Some of the people who lived in the area sold animals, food, and supplies to the many wagon trains that passed through.

Western Nebraska was part of Mexico until the Mexican War ended in 1848, when it became part of the United States. Adding the new land paved the way for the Gold Rush travelers and other western settlers.

In May 28, 1854, Nebraska and Kansas became territories with the passage of the Kansas-Nebraska Act. (Many areas were territories before they became states.) The Nebraska Territory reached all the way up to the Canadian border until the Dakota Territory was created from the northern part in 1863.

Today, Nebraska is the only state in the Union that has only one house in its government. All other states have two, like the federal government's Senate and House of Representatives of Congress. Nebraska's one-house government is called "unicameral" from Latin words meaning "one chamber."

1. *Which event took place before Louis and Clark's expedition?*
   Ⓐ Gold Rush
   Ⓑ Mexican War
   Ⓒ Louisiana Purchase
   Ⓓ Kansas-Nebraska Act

2. *When did Western Nebraska become part of the United States?*
   Ⓐ 1803
   Ⓑ 1806
   Ⓒ 1848
   Ⓓ 1854

3. *Nebraska is unique among all states because it*
   Ⓐ has only one house in its government.
   Ⓑ was part of the Louisiana Purchase.
   Ⓒ included the Oregon Trail.
   Ⓓ extended to the Canadian border.

4. *This passage is **best** described as*
   Ⓐ an imaginative fairy tale from long ago.
   Ⓑ historical fiction with a plot and characters.
   Ⓒ a myth that explains the origin of something.
   Ⓓ a nonfiction essay that explains a topic.

5. *A territory is*
   Ⓐ the same as a state.
   Ⓑ not the same as a state.
   Ⓒ better than a state.
   Ⓓ part of the federal government.

Scoring Sheet

As you did with other practice standardized tests in this book, go back over your score. See what you did right and what you need to improve. Then take the test again, using what you learned to correct any problems you had.

1. Ⓐ Ⓑ Ⓒ Ⓓ
2. Ⓐ Ⓑ Ⓒ Ⓓ
3. Ⓐ Ⓑ Ⓒ Ⓓ
4. Ⓐ Ⓑ Ⓒ Ⓓ
5. Ⓐ Ⓑ Ⓒ Ⓓ

ANSWERS
1.C, 2. C, 3. A, 4. D, 5. B

CHAPTER 7: **Multiple-Choice Standardized Tests**

CHAPTER

8

Kiara does well on standardized tests
that have short-answer questions.
What's her secret? It's in this chapter!

Short-Answer
Standardized
Tests

What are Short-Answer Standardized Tests?

Short-answer tests take two forms: *incomplete sentences* and *brief responses.*

✶*Incomplete sentences:* You are asked to fill in the missing part in a sentence. It may be a word or a phrase. There will be a blank in the sentence. You may be asked to write on the test or on a separate answer sheet.

✶ *Brief response:* You are asked to write a few sentences. You may write on the test or on a separate answer sheet.

Short-answer tests are used in many standardized tests. You'll often find them in state standardized tests. In standardized math tests, they test your ability to work with numbers. You might be asked to add, subtract, multiply, or divide. They find out if you remember math terms such as *factor* and *prime number*, too. In social studies and science standardized tests, short-answer tests check your knowledge of facts, data, and theories. They also see how well you can follow the steps in a process. In language arts standardized tests, they see how well you can read and interpret a passage. You'll be given a short story, fable, myth, or nonfiction passage. Then you'll have to write sentences about the reading.

know the facts

Below are some sample items from a standardized short-answer test in science and social studies. **FILL IN THE ANSWERS NOW.**

1. *The largest body in our solar system is the* _____.

2. *The* _____ *was the period in European history at the close of the Middle Ages, around the 1400s. It was a cultural rebirth. Many great writers and artists lived during this time.*

3. *The two factors for 5 are* _____ *and* _____.

4. *Name the three branches of the U.S. federal government.*

   _____

   _____

   _____

5. *To make sure that no part of government had too much power,*

   the Founding Fathers set up a system of _____

   _____.

ANSWERS
1. Sun; 2. Renaissance; 3. 5, 1;
4. judicial, executive, and legislative; 5. checks and balances

You learned how to do your best on multiple-choice standardized tests. In the same way, you can learn skills for succeeding on short-answer standardized tests. *Use the methods below.*

Study Well.

Short-answer standardized tests are most often recall tests.

Recall = Remember

You are being tested on knowing specific details. This means that you must recall facts. You can't use process of elimination to find the most likely answer, as you can with multiple-choice questions. As a result, you must memorize information to do well on these short-answer tests.

Short-answer standardized tests can also ask you to interpret information and draw conclusions. This is most common on the reading parts of some standardized tests. To study for these tests, *take practice tests*. Learn the critical thinking skills you will need.

HERE ARE SOME GOOD WAYS TO LEARN FACTS FOR STANDARDIZED TESTS.

* *Make flashcards.* Write important dates, facts, and ideas on the front of each card. Write details about each date, facts, or idea on the back.

* *Use the flashcards.* They're useless if they sit in the bottom of your backpack! Be sure to practice a lot with the flashcards.

* *Write summaries.* Make up your own lists of facts. Writing the facts helps you remember them. Reading the summaries reinforces what you learned.

* *Anticipate questions.* Be a test detective. Try to figure out what the teacher will ask on a classroom test. Here are your clues: facts the teacher wrote on the board, information the teacher emphasized in class, big ideas in your textbook.

Do a Brain Dump.

In Chapter 6, you learned easy ways to relax during a standardized test. One good way is to jot down facts before you start answering questions. This is called a "brain dump." It's a silly name for a great idea! Here's how to do it.

Skim the standardized test. (When you skim, you read really fast. You look for the main idea.) As you read each question, jot down any facts that come to mind. You'll probably be able to use many of these facts as you fill in the blanks. Even if you can't, you've gotten your brain into "standardized test mode." You see that you know a lot. This helps you relax.

details! details! details!

Read Carefully.

Be sure you understand the statement. If you need to, say the statement in your own words. Underline key words. These are the words that help you know what you're being asked. Look for tricky words that are often misread like **through** and **though** or **quiet** and **quite**.

Follow the Rules of Writing.

Be sure to follow the rules of standard written English. For example, capitalize the first word in a sentence and all proper nouns. Use a period at the end of a complete sentence.

Try to Fill in Every Question.

Try not to leave any questions blank.

What should you do if you don't know an answer? Skip the question and return to it at the end of the test, if you have time. You might have remembered the answer or found a clue in another question.

Check Your Answers

Use common sense.
If an answer doesn't seem logical, it's probably wrong. Reread the question.

Write Clearly.

Write short, direct sentences.
Don't make the scorer hunt for the answer. Give reasons, examples, and proofs to show that you understand the subject. Also, **be sure your writing is legible.** That means it can be read. If your handwriting is messy, print instead.

be neat and complete

Try what you learned now!

Complete the following sample standardized *Reading Test. As you did in Chapter 7, try to get as close to standardized test conditions as you can.* This means to sit alone in a quiet place. Make sure the television and your cell phone are turned off. Set aside 25 minutes for the test. Write down your time when you start. Write down your time when you end.

sit alone in a **quiet** place

DIRECTIONS: *Answer all questions from this part.* Each correct answer will receive 5 points. ***Write your answers in the lines provided.*** You have 25 minutes to complete this part of the test.

Practice Reading Test 1

The Daydreamer
A story from India

Once a merchant was going to market with his pots of oil arranged on a flat basket. He hired Yesha for two annas to carry the basket. And as he went along, Yesha thought: "With one anna I will buy food and with the other I will buy chickens. The chickens will grow up and multiply, and then I will sell some of the fowls and eggs, and with the money I will buy goats. And when the goats increase, I will sell some and buy cows. Then I will trade some of the calves for buffaloes. When the buffaloes breed, I will sell some and buy land and start cultivation. Then I will marry and have children. I will hurry back from my work in the fields. My wife will bring me water, and I will have a rest. My children will say to me, "Father, be quick and wash your hands for dinner," but I will shake my head and say, "No, no, not yet!"
And as he thought about it he really shook his head, and the basket fell to the ground, and all the pots of oil were smashed!

Then the merchant yelled at Yesha. The merchant said, "You must pay two rupees for the oil and one anna for the pots."

Yesha replied, "I have lost much more than that!"

The merchant asked, "How can that be?"

Yesha explained, "With my wages, I was going to get fowls and then goats and then oxen and buffaloes and land. I spilled the basket because I shook my head. All the pots of oil smashed."
The merchant roared with laughter and said, "Well, I have made up the account, and I find that our losses are equal, so we will say that we are equal." And so saying they went their ways laughing.

Adapted from *Folklore of the Santal Parganas* by Cecil Henry Bompas .

1. **_Annas and rupees are_**

_____

_____

2. **_What is Yesha's plan?_**

_____

_____

3. **_Who is the daydreamer?_**

_____

_____

4. **_At the end of the story, the merchant laughs because_**

_____

_____

5. **_At the end of the story, Yesha laughs because_**

_____

_____

6. **_What lesson does this story teach?_**

_____

_____

POSSIBLE ANSWERS: 1. money **2.** He wants to use his small, one-day's pay to build his entire life. **3.** Yesha **4.** he finds Yesha's plans silly. **5.** he realizes that his plans are silly. **6.** Don't count your chickens before they hatch.

DIRECTIONS: *Answer all questions from this part.* Each correct answer will receive 5 points. *Write your answers in the lines provided.* You have 25 minutes to complete this part of the test.

Practice Reading Test 2

The Eagle and the Owl
A story from France

The eagle and the owl entered into a treaty with each another, each taking a solemn oath that neither would ever harm the chicks of the other. "But do you know what my chicks look like?" asked the mother owl. She feared that the eagle might attack them by mistake.

"No, I do not know what they look like," said the eagle. "Describe them, so that I will know to spare them."

"They cannot be mistaken for any other bird," returned the proud mother owl. "They are small and ever so beautiful, by far the prettiest of any baby bird."

One evening, while scouting for food, the eagle came upon a nest filled with screeching baby birds. "Surely these do not belong to my friend, the owl," said the eagle. "No, for hers are things of great beauty, but these are hideous, ugly creatures." And he swept down and devoured them every one.

Returning to her nest, the mother owl found only the feet of her offspring. "How can the eagle have broken his promise?" she asked herself in grief. "Didn't he hear me describe my little ones as the most beautiful chicks of all?"

Retold from a fable in verse by Jean de La Fontaine (1621-1695).

1. *The mother owl describes her babies as*

_____

_____

2. *The eagle describes the owl's babies as*

_____

_____

3. *Why does the eagle eat the baby owls?*

_____

_____

4. *Hideous means*

_____

_____

5. *The moral of the story is:*
   Every mother thinks that her own children are

_____

_____

POSSIBLE ANSWERS: 1. beautiful **2.** ugly **3.** Eagles eat owls. The eagle doesn't think these owls are her friend's babies. **4.** very ugly **5.** the prettiest of all.

TAKE A TEN-MINUTE BREAK.
Then go back over the test. See what questions you missed.
Reread the passage to find the answers.

Think about the problems you had. What kinds of mistakes did you make?

.... 1. misread the passage

.... 2. didn't know the words

.... 3. worked too fast

.... 4. misunderstood the passage

.... 5. used the wrong words

Think about these things when you take your next standardized test.

CHAPTER
9

Writing
Essays
on Standardized Tests

WRITER WILLIAM GOLDMAN SAID:

"The easiest thing to do on earth is *not* write."

Writing is a lot easier if you follow a few simple steps.

There are only five steps. **HERE THEY ARE:**

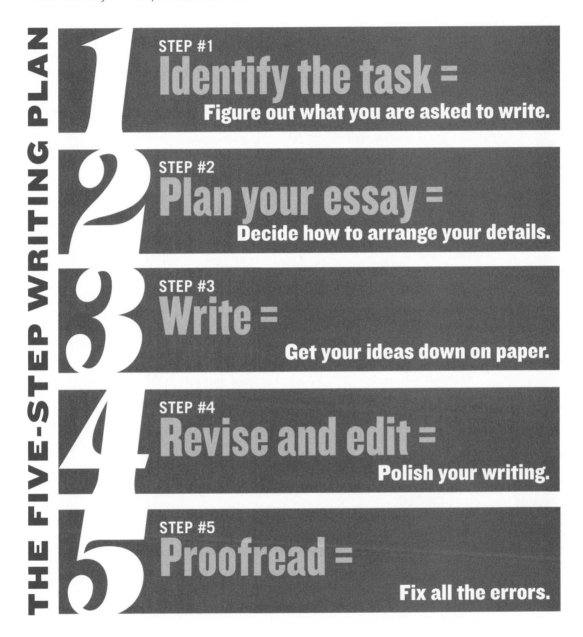

THE FIVE-STEP WRITING PLAN

1

STEP #1
Identify the task =
Figure out what you are asked to write.

2

STEP #2
Plan your essay =
Decide how to arrange your details.

3

STEP #3
Write =
Get your ideas down on paper.

4

STEP #4
Revise and edit =
Polish your writing.

5

STEP #5
Proofread =
Fix all the errors.

This five-step process works especially well when you write essays on standardized tests. That's because your time is limited on a standardized test. You have to get to work right away. Learning these five steps helps you feel less nervous, too. That's because you have a plan.

Standardized writing tests ask you to respond to a **prompt**. "Prompt" is just a fancy word for the writing assignment. The prompt will be a question or a statement. First, read the prompt carefully to figure out what you have to do. You will have to tell a story, explain something, or argue a point. *Look for key words that identify the type of writing. Study the chart below.*

TYPE OF WRITING	USE	SAMPLE PROMPT	KEY WORD(S)
Tell a story	characters, setting, suspense	*One day, a spaceship landed on the school parking lot . . . Finish this story.*	story
Explain something	details, facts, examples	*Rules help make us safer. Create three new school rules. Then explain how these rules would help people.*	explain
Argue a point	details, facts, examples	*Suppose that your school has decided that all students must learn a foreign language in school. Write an essay for or against this idea.*	for or against

look for **key words**

organize!

STEP #2: Plan Your Essay

Take a few minutes to plan what you're going to write.

HERE ARE SOME GREAT WAYS TO PLAN:

BRAINSTORM: *List ideas on your topic.* Write fast. Don't worry about spelling. Just try to get your ideas down on paper.

OUTLINE: See how your ideas fit together. *Ask yourself: "How are these ideas linked? What should come first? What should come last?"* You don't have to use all your ideas. You can add new ones, too. Then put your ideas into an outline.

TRY IT NOW WITH THIS TOPIC: THINK OF YOUR FAVORITE ANIMAL. EXPLAIN WHY THIS ANIMAL MAKES A GOOD PET.

HERE'S A SAMPLE LIST:

<u>Dogs</u>
fun
rescue dogs
clean
guide dogs
helpful
playing catch with my dog Fido
cute
friendship
German shepherds

HERE'S A SAMPLE:

I. Introduction
II. First main idea: DOGS ARE FUN.
   A. Example: *Playing catch with my dog Fido in the park.*
   B. Example: *Cuddling Fido on the couch.*
III. Second main idea: DOGS ARE HELPFUL.
   A. Example: *Dogs help blind people be more independent.*
   B. Example: *Dogs help rescue injured hikers.*
IV. Conclusion

HERE ARE SOME DIFFERENT WAYS TO ARRANGE YOUR IDEAS:

TYPE OF WRITING	WAYS TO ARRANGE IDEAS
Tell a story	time order (beginning to end)
Explain something	alike and different cause and effect problem and solution
Argue a point	most-to-least important reasons least-to-most important reasons

STEP #3: **Write**

Write your essay. Most people start at the beginning, but you don't have to. If you get stuck for a good opening, skip to the next paragraph. Plan your time so you can go back to the opening and finish it. Your goal is to get your ideas down on paper.

Make your writing interesting and fun to read. Remember: The scorer has to read a lot of essays.

HERE ARE SOME WAYS TO MAKE YOUR WRITING STAND OUT.

* Use vivid words.
For example, don't call something *red*.
Instead, call it *strawberry*, *scarlet*, *ruby*, or *cherry*.

* Describe things with exact language.
Don't say that something is *large*.
Instead, say it is *as big as the school cafeteria*.

* Add words that appeal to the five senses.
Say, the table was *sticky like cotton candy*.

STEP #4: Revise and Edit

WHEN YOU REVISE AND EDIT, YOU:

* Add missing details.

* Add vivid words that make your writing interesting.

* Add words that appeal to the five senses.
This helps your reader visualize your people, places, and things.

* Cross out details that are off the topic.

* Move words that are in the wrong place.

* Correct errors in spelling, punctuation, capitalization, and grammar.

On some standardized writing tests, you may not have time to go back to revise and edit. If so, revise and edit as you write.

**TO REVISE AND EDIT, READ YOUR
PAPER ALL THE WAY THROUGH.**
*Use a checklist to help you focus
your ideas.* Here is a sample checklist:

1. *Have I answered the prompt?*

2. *Does my writing have a clear
   method of organization?*

3. *Do I start each paragraph with a topic
   sentence that states the main idea?*

4. *Do I include major points?*

5. *Have I included details and
   examples in the essay?*

6. *Have I included dialogue in a story?*

7. *Do I link ideas in a logical way?*

8. *Do I end with a conclusion that
   sums up the main ideas?*

9. *Is my writing entertaining
   and enjoyable to read?*

10. *Have I crossed off any information that
    is not on the topic?*

11. *Have I corrected spelling errors?*

12. *Have I corrected capitalization errors?*

13. *Have I corrected punctuation errors?*

14. *Have I corrected grammar errors?*

15. *Can my handwriting be read easily?*

STEP #5: **Proofread**

Always leave yourself time to proofread. ***Don't skip this step!*** You only need three or four minutes. It is time well spent.

correct

careless

mist~~eaks~~

mistakes

Sample Essay

PROMPT: SUPPOSE THAT YOU WERE AN OBJECT IN THE CLASSROOM. WHAT WOULD YOU BE AND WHY?

Write about 200 words on this topic. You have 20 minutes to write.

I'm so glad that I'm the blackboard! Being a blackboard makes me the center of attention

  INTRODUCTION   **TOPIC SENTENCE**

because I help people. Not to brag, but I am the most useful and good-looking part

            1ST MAIN IDEA

of the classroom.

First, I like attention and because I am the blackboard, people always look at me. That's

         TOPIC SENTENCE

because so much important information is written on me, including homework and classwork.

    2ND MAIN IDEA

Kids learn a lot from me, too, like math, science, and language arts. Just yesterday Ms. Coletti

       EXAMPLE

had Feruk and Neveah come to me, the board, to do multiplication problems.

       DETAILS

Last but not least, I'm very special because you can use me over and over. When people

       TOPIC SENTENCE

want to write something new on me, they can. They wipe an eraser over my surface and I'm

   EXAMPLE   **EXAMPLE**

all clean. People can clean me with a wet sponge, too. The cool water feels good on my dry

       EXAMPLE   **DETAILS**

slate skin. I dry very fast, so I'm ready to use in a few minutes. I'm very handsome when I'm

all wet. I turn sleek and shiny like a wet seal.

    DETAILS

There's only one drawback to being a blackboard: being scratched. Blackboards never itch,

       CONCLUSION

so why do people scratch us? We blackboards hate it! I squeal when you scratch me.

Everyone gets goose bumps when they hear my screech. But overall, I am very glad that

I'm a blackboard rather than the dusty piece of chalk or the boring clock.

Sample Prompts

Below are some writing prompts. They are in different formats from standardized tests. **Try them all!**

READ THIS TOPIC CAREFULLY BEFORE YOU BEGIN WRITING.

WRITING SITUATION: *Think about a chore you do at home. It might be washing the dishes, walking the dog, or cleaning your room, for example.*

DIRECTIONS FOR WRITING: *Before you begin to write, brainstorm the steps you follow to complete this chore. List some sequence words to help you explain the steps in the correct order.*

NOW WRITE THE ESSAY EXPLAINING HOW TO DO THIS CHORE CORRECTLY.

You may use this space for prewriting notes. However, only the lined pages of your answer folder will be scored. This sheet must be returned with all test material.

Remember that you have a time limit of 35 minutes. Use the space below for notes.

Write an essay explaining why respect matters. Also describe how to show respect to people. You have 20 minutes.

Choose a teacher who made a positive impact on your life. Think of some ways the teacher changed your life. Explain how the teacher made your life better.

Imagine that you had no television, radio, movies, video games, or iPods for a week. Think of some activities you could like to do instead. Write an essay to explain what you can do to have fun for a week without media.

5

HERE IS PART OF THE SPEECH THAT MUSICIAN BILLY JOEL GAVE AT THE GRADUATION CEREMONY AT THE BERKLEE COLLEGE OF MUSIC IN 1993. READ THIS PARAGRAPH CAREFULLY. THEN ANSWER THE QUESTION THAT FOLLOWS.

"I can't think of one person I've ever met who didn't like some type of music. More than art, more than literature, music is universally accessible. For whatever reason, not all people are born with the particular gift that we have: the gift of being able to express ourselves through music. And, believe me, it is a gift. But people who don't have this ability still need to find a way to give a voice to what they're thinking and feeling, to find something that connects them with others. As human beings, we need to know that we are not alone, that we are not crazy or that we are all completely out of our minds, that there are other people out there who feel as we do, who live as we do, who love as we do, who are like us."

Summarize Billy Joel's argument. Then agree or disagree with what he says. Give examples that support your opinion.

6

Think of a book you like a lot. It may be your favorite book, but does not have to be. Write a review of the book telling why it is so good. Convince your audience to read the book.

7

Should there be a dress code at your school? Argue for or against.

try them all!

8

Some people argue that school should be in session year-round, with only a few holidays off. People in favor of full-year school claim that kids will learn more. They won't forget information over the summer and will have time in school to study subjects in greater depth, too. People against full-year school argue that kids need a long summer vacation to rest. They need this time with their families, too. They also say that full-year school will cost too much. Argue for or against full-year school.

10

Write a story about yourself as a superhero.

11

Your class grew some plants as a science project. One day you looked at your plant. Something really strange had grown there. Tell the story of your plant.

9

Suppose that you had your own television show. Tell a story about one episode in the show.

12

You were playing with your cat, Mittens. You spoke to your cat. She answered you! Write a story about the conversation you had with your cat.

CHAPTER
10

Now it's time to put together everything you've learned. Take these practice tests. Pretend that you are taking an actual test. Sit in a quiet place. Take each test in one sitting. Time yourself. Then score yourself. See what areas need improvement. Reread the parts of the book that cover those skills.

Practice
Tests

Test #1

Write your answers and essay on a separate sheet of paper.

Three Precepts

A hunter once caught a bird that was very clever and able to speak seventy languages. The bird said to its captor, "Set me free, and I will teach you three precepts which will be of great use to you."

"Tell me these rules, and I will set you free," said the hunter. "Promise me first," retorted the clever bird, "that you will keep your promise and in truth set me free."

When the man swore to keep his promise, the bird said, "My first precept is: Never regret anything that has happened. My second rule of conduct is: Never believe anything you are told that is impossible and beyond belief. My third precept is: Never try to reach something that is unattainable."

Having spoken thus, the man opened his hand and let the captive bird fly away.

The bird sat down on the top of a tree and mockingly called to the man below, "Stupid man, you did allow me to fly away not knowing that a precious pearl was hidden in my body, a pearl that is the cause of my great wisdom."

When the bird-catcher heard these words he greatly regretted having allowed the bird to fly away, and rushing up to the tree, he tried to climb it. Failing in his efforts, he fell down and broke his legs.

The bird laughed, saying, "Fool! Not an hour has passed since I taught you three wise precepts, and you have already forgotten them. I told you never to regret anything that was past, and you did repent having set me free. I told you never to believe anything that was evidently beyond belief, and you were credulous enough to believe that I actually carried a costly pearl in my body. I am only a poor wild bird always searching for food. And finally, I advised you never to strive in vain after the unattainable. While you tried to catch a bird with your hands, and are now lying below with broken legs. Alas, there are many men as unwise as yourself." The bird flew away in search of nourishment.

1. *Read the sentence from the passage.*

The bird said to its captor, "Set me free, and I will teach you three precepts which will be of great use to you."

*Which of these is the meaning of **precepts** as it is used in this sentence?*
(A) skills
(B) laws
(C) principles
(D) principals

2. *The bird makes the hunter promise to set him free before he offers his three precepts because the bird knows the hunter*
(A) is very intelligent and honorable.
(B) always betrays animals, especially birds.
(C) cannot be trusted because he is not wise.
(D) realizes the value of the three precepts.

3. *Which event happens first in the story?*
(A) The hunter captures a bird.
(B) The bird speaks to a hunter.
(C) The hunter climbs a tree.
(D) The bird flies away.

4. *The hunter climbs the tree to*
(A) escape from the aggressive bird that frightens him.
(B) get a better view of the landscape and find other birds.
(C) think about what he learned from the shrewd bird.
(D) capture the bird, kill it, and get its treasure.

5. *Which statement is true?*
(A) The bird has swallowed a rare pearl.
(B) The bird tricks the hunter.
(C) The hunter will never go after birds again.
(D) All birds can fly, but only some can talk.

6. *A credulous person is*
Ⓐ very honorable
Ⓑ somewhat talented
Ⓒ easily tricked
Ⓓ badly injured

7. *You can conclude that this is a fable because it*
Ⓐ has a surprising and funny ending.
Ⓑ is very ancient and comes from another culture.
Ⓒ teaches a lesson though talking animals.
Ⓓ is true to life and explains things well.

8. *Restate the three precepts in your own words.*

9. *Is the bird wise? Why or why not?*

10. *Write one more precept to live by.*

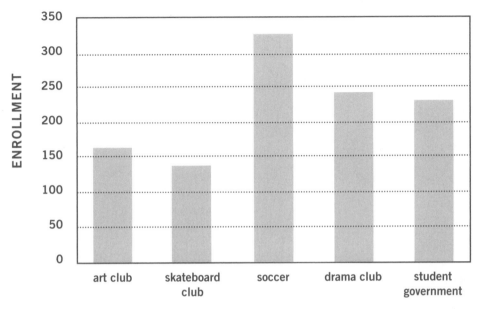

ENROLLMENT IN EXTRACURRICULAR ACTIVITIES
AT EASTSIDE ELEMENTARY SCHOOL

ENROLLMENT

INTRODUCTORY COURSES

11. **Which activity has the most students enrolled in it?**
Ⓐ art club
Ⓑ soccer
Ⓒ drama club
Ⓓ student government

12. **Which activity has the least students enrolled in it?**
Ⓐ drama club
Ⓑ student government
Ⓒ art club
Ⓓ skateboard club

13. **About how many students are enrolled in drama club?**
Ⓐ 240
Ⓑ 160
Ⓒ 340
Ⓓ 190

14. **Where is Carson City located?**
Ⓐ Reno
Ⓑ California
Ⓒ Nevada
Ⓓ Washoe Lake

15. **Which main road will take you to Humboldt-Toiyabe National Forest?**
Ⓐ Route 208
Ⓑ Route 395
Ⓒ Route 446
Ⓓ Route 95

Writing

Choose one of the topics and answer in 200–300 words.

IMAGINE THAT A NEW FAMILY HAS MOVED TO YOUR TOWN.
Explain what parts of your town they should see.
Tell what makes these places special.

CHOOSE A SUBJECT OR CLASS THAT YOUR SCHOOL DOES NOT OFFER.
Write a letter to persuade the school board to offer this class.

TELL A STORY ABOUT A DAY WHEN EVERYTHING WENT WRONG.

Test #2

DIRECTIONS: This test has 15 questions.
Write your answers on a separate sheet of paper.

Fire!

Fires have burned across the earth for millions of years and continue to do so today. Evidence of fires that burned in the past exists in petrified trees that lived long ago and have, over many years, turned hard like a rock. Some petrified trees have fossilized charcoal called fusain in their trunks. Fusain shows that the trees were once in the path of a fire. On a living tree, burn marks are called fire scars. Native Americans used fire to help with hunting more than 4,000 years ago.

Fires occur naturally with the help of lightning and lava, but humans start approximately 90 percent of wildland fires. Most times, they start fires accidentally. Lightning and lava start the remaining 10 percent of wildland fires. Lightning is like a gigantic spark between a negatively charged lower cloud and the positively charged Earth. Lightning strikes the Earth about 100 times each second. Lightning temperatures can sometimes reach more than 50,000° F! That's more than five times hotter than the sun's surface! Imagine what happens when lightning strikes a field of dry grass.

Some pinecones, called serotinous cones, rely on fire to help them open so they can release their seeds. Although fire can benefit an ecosystem, it may threaten human life or property. If the weather conditions are very dry or windy, fire burns much faster. Also, a fire burning near homes may damage those houses. Smoke can also be a cause of damage to homes. In a building, smoke smells unpleasant, leaves ashes, and impacts human health. In addition, smoke can make it difficult to see when driving.

Source: National Park Service

1. *Read the following sentence from the passage.*

Evidence of fires that burned in the past exists in petrified trees that lived long ago and have, over many years, turned hard like a rock.

Petrified *is used in this sentence to mean*
Ⓐ terrified.
Ⓑ turned to rock.
Ⓒ trusting.
Ⓓ ancient.

2. *How do most fires start?*
Ⓐ during thunderstorms
Ⓑ from burning lava
Ⓒ as a result of lightning
Ⓓ from human carelessness

3. *You can conclude that lightning strikes*
Ⓐ rarely.
Ⓑ only in forests.
Ⓒ often.
Ⓓ trees, not people.

4. *Which statement is true?*
Ⓐ All fires must be stopped to protect our precious natural resources.
Ⓑ Scientists are developing ways to stop lightning from striking forests.
Ⓒ The sun is much hotter than a lightning strike.
Ⓓ Wildland fires can help some forests stay healthy and productive.

5. *You can infer that*
Ⓐ most fires are started on purpose.
Ⓑ marshes and swamps can burn.
Ⓒ fire causes the most damage to pine trees.
Ⓓ scientists do not know much about fire.

6. *All of the following are negative effects of fire but*
Ⓐ reseeding pinecones.
Ⓑ damage to homes.
Ⓒ harm to our health.
Ⓓ messy ashes all over.

7. **You can conclude that firefighters are most concerned with**
Ⓐ getting the fire under control.
Ⓑ keeping people safe.
Ⓒ protecting property.
Ⓓ conserving the forest.

8. **On a living tree, burn marks are called** _____.

9. **Explain one way that fires benefit forests.**

10. **Write a sentence explaining how you could help prevent forest fires.**

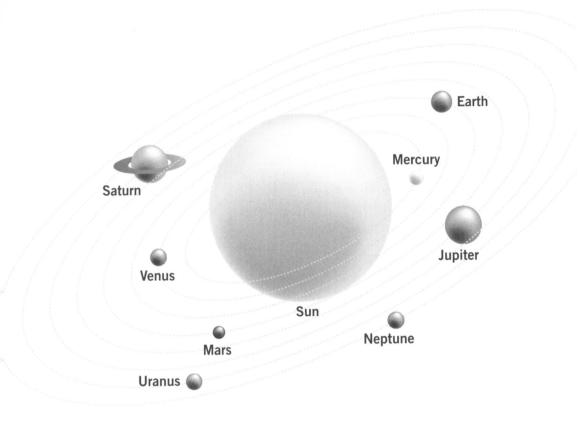

11. **Which planet is closest to the Sun?**
Ⓐ Venus
Ⓑ Earth
Ⓒ Saturn
Ⓓ Mars

12. **What is the correct order of planets, moving from the sun outward?**
Ⓐ Neptune, Uranus, Saturn, Jupiter, Mars
Ⓑ Mars, Uranus, Jupiter, Saturn, Neptune
Ⓒ Saturn, Neptune, Mars, Jupiter, Uranus
Ⓓ Mars, Jupiter, Saturn, Uranus, Neptune

13. **Which planet is largest?**
Ⓐ the Sun
Ⓑ Jupiter
Ⓒ Neptune
Ⓓ Uranus

14. **The new movie theater will cost seventy-two million dollars. This number can also be written as**
   Ⓐ $70,200
   Ⓑ $72,000
   Ⓒ $72,000,000
   Ⓓ $70,200,000

15. **6794 − 3609 =**
   Ⓐ 3185
   Ⓑ 2185
   Ⓒ 3195
   Ⓓ 3085

Writing

Choose one of the topics and answer in 200−300 words.

EXPLAIN WHY IT IS IMPORTANT TO BE A GOOD READER.

IMAGINE THAT YOU COULD TRAVEL IN A TIME MACHINE BACK TO THE PAST. *Choose a time and place to visit.*
Then write a story about your adventures there.

SUPPOSE THAT YOUR SCHOOL IS DECIDING IF THEY SHOULD DISCONTINUE ALL FIELD TRIPS. *Write a letter to the local newspaper for or against canceling all field trips.*

Answers

Test 1

1. C
2. C
3. A
4. D
5. B
6. A
7. C

POSSIBLE ANSWERS

8. Rule #1: Don't feel bad about your mistakes.
Rule #2: Don't believe things that sound unbelievable.
Rule #3: Don't try to grab something you can't reach.

9. The bird is wise because his rules are sensible. They are good rules to live by.

10. Treat other people as you would like them to treat you.

11. B
12. D
13. A
14. C
15. D

Test 2

1. B
2. D
3. C
4. A
5. A
6. D
7. B

POSSIBLE ANSWERS

8. fire scars

9. Fire helps some plants, such as pine trees, reseed.

10. I would make sure to put out my campfire when camping.

11. C
12. D
13. B
14. C
15. A

CHAPTER 10: **Practice Tests**